A Cinema Like Nothing : 100 Years of Bollywood

Diptarup Das

Introduction

The Indian film industry stands above most other national cinemas due to its local focus yet enormous size. Although gaining more and more international popularity, the main audience for this cinematic titan resides within India, and while this may seem a restrictive quality, the fact that India is the second most populated country in the world, combined with the local focus of Indian cinemas (in 2012 foreign imports only filled 9% of the total film box office), Indian cinema has grown to become one of the largest film industries in the world. Although the film industry is widely known as 'Bollywood', this term actually only refers to the Hindi-language films produced through the studios in Mumbai (Bombay), only one part of the incredible spectrum of Indian films, albeit the largest. The origins of cinema can be traced back to the French Lumière Brothers. Unveiling their first short films in 1895, these revolutionary filmmakers tempted the world with a new form of entertainment. In 1896, the brothers toured their works to India for the first time, hosting a screening in Mumbai Watson Hotel. Reported as the 'Miracle of the Century' by *The Times of India*, it was not long until converted film fanatics started to emerge in the then British governed India. Through experimenting with techniques and technologies, early filmmaker Hiralal Sen made the first Indian short film in 1898. 1912 then saw the first screened Indian silent film, *Shree Pundalik*, directed by Dadasaheb Torne. Outside help was used however, with the film shot by British cinematographers and the negatives sent to London to be processed. It was the next year, 1913, which saw the first truly authentic Indian film being screened: Dadasaheb Phalke's *Raja Harishchandra*, and thus Indian cinema was born.

Since these early beginnings India's film industry has continued to flourish, growing in popularity, size and reach. There are many factors for this ongoing growth, one of them being the affordability of cinema in the country. From the early days onwards, India cinema venues have made films accessible to the wider public, providing cheap admission, with convenient extras being sold as buyable additions, not inbuilt in the price. With the vast economic gap that is found in India, this factor has allowed film to become an art form for the people, not just for the upper class.

Interestingly, in the late 1920s the Britishgovernment tried to promote UK film in India in an attempt to overtake the growingAmerican cinema, and created the Indian Cinematograph Enquiry Committee. This programme failed with this aim however, with the committee favouring Indianproduced films; it seemed that nothing could stop the growth of this national movement. With technology advancements, sound and dialogue became more and more implemented in Indian films throughout the 1930s, leading to a surge of song and dance in films, such as in *Indrasabha* and *Devi Devyani*. This element would take a strong hold in Hindi cinema, and is a renowned quality found in many Bollywood films being made today.

Another influential factor in Bollywood's growth was India's independence in 1947. Proud in becoming an autonomous country, national cinema experienced a Golden Era from the 1940s to the 1960s. This era saw directors such as Satyajit Ray, Guru Dutt, Raj Kapoor andVijay Bhatt create a wide range of classic films, further establishing and redefining Indian film. It was these influential filmmakers who paved the pathway for the future of Bollywood, and its present day position as one of the largest film industries in the world.

One of the most flourishing cinema industries found today is in India. But the pioneers of the industry were actually foreigners. In 1896, the Lumiere brothers demonstrated the art of cinema when they screened Cinematography consisting of six short films to an enthusiastic audience in Bombay. The success of these films led to the screening of films by James B. Stewart and Ted Hughes.

In 1897, Save Dada made two short films, but the fathers of Indian cinema were Dada Saheb Phalke who in 1913 made the first feature length silent film and Ardeshir Irani who in 1931 made India's first talking film.

With the demise of the silent era and the advent of the talkies, the main source for inspiration for films came from mythological texts. Films were produced in Hindi, Tamil, Telugu and Bengali. Mythology flourished more in South India where its social conservative morals equated film acting to prostitution. But by the 1930's, word had spread around the world about the vibrant film industry in India and foreigners with stars in their eyes landed upon Bombay shores.

One of these was Mary Evans, a young Australian girl who could do stunts. She could, with no effort, lift a man and throw him across the room. She wore Zorro-like masks and used a whip when necessary. She changed her name to Nadia and was affectionately known by the audience as Fearless Nadia and that name stuck with her through the ages. Even though she did not speak any of the native tongues, her career spanned from the 1930's to 1959. She had a huge cult following. The press and critics did not appreciate her; however, the audiences could not get enough of her stunt theatrics.

Following on Nadia's heels in 1940, Florence Esekiel, a teenager from Baghdad, arrived in Bombay and was soon given the screen name of Nadira. She played the love interest in a Dilip Kumar film who at the time was a leading heartthrob. She moved on to playing bitchy parts and was forever type cast as a 'vamp' – the temptress, the bad girl. She gradually slipped into mother roles. One of her last appearances was in Ismail Merchant film *Cotton Mary*.

There were also notable male actors who made a mark on the screen. One of them was Bob Christo, who was another Australian. He came to India because he had seen a picture of the actress Parveen Babi and ended up actually being in a film with her. He specialized in villain and henchman roles.

Another notable actor is Tom Alter who has played the foreigner who does not speak the language, although he is fluent in Hindi and Urdu, even reciting poems in Urdu on the stage. He was raised in Mussourie, India.

And then we must not forget Helen. A Franco-Burmese refuge who broke all norms, she embodied sexuality and filled the roles that other actresses with conservative views shunned. She was widely sought after for her dance or 'item numbers' as they are called today. However she stayed within the code of decency wearing body stockings all the times. She did venture out of this zone by doing a few serious roles.

In the 1920's Franz Austen, a German from Munich who could not utter one word of Hindi, came to Bombay and directed 57 blockbuster films. His films were on the scale of those made by Cecil B. DeMille. He drew his inspiration from episodes of the Mahabharata and Ramayana, his early silent films were richer than most that were made at the time.

In 1947, When India gained its independence, mythological and historical stories were being replaced by social reformist films focusing on the lives of the lower classes, the dowry system and prostitution. This brought a new wave of filmmakers to the forefront such as Bimal Roy and Satyajit Ray among others. In the 1960's, inspired by social and cinematic changes in the US and Europe, India's new wave was founded, offering a greater sense of realism to the public and getting recognition abroad, but the industry at large churned out 'masala' films with a mesh of genres including action, comedy, melodrama punctuated with songs and dances and relying on the songs and the stars to sell their films.

Today there is a growing movement to make Indian cinema more real - a group of young filmmakers like Anurag Kashyap, Anand Gandhi, and Gyan Correa, whose film *The Good Road* is this year's contender for the Oscars. There are now more large investments from corporate houses and a more structured industry funding independent cinema and making it a viable and profitable business.

There has never been a more favorable time for Indian cinema than today. With a vibrant creative community, new technology and investment interest, we are on the verge of seeing Indian cinema transcend its national borders to project India's socio-political and economic influence around the world.

A Brief History of Indian Cinema

When Dadasaheb Phalke, the father of Indian Cinema, released his epochal feature film Raja Harishchandra on 3rd May 1913, it is unlikely that either the exhibitors or the pioneer film maker realized they were unleashing a mass entertainment medium that would hold millions in sway for the next hundred years. The French might have introduced the concept of moving images, but little did anyone know that India would one day become the largest film industry in the world. It's a miracle that Indian cinema has withstood the test of time despite the vast cultural differences in the past 100 years.

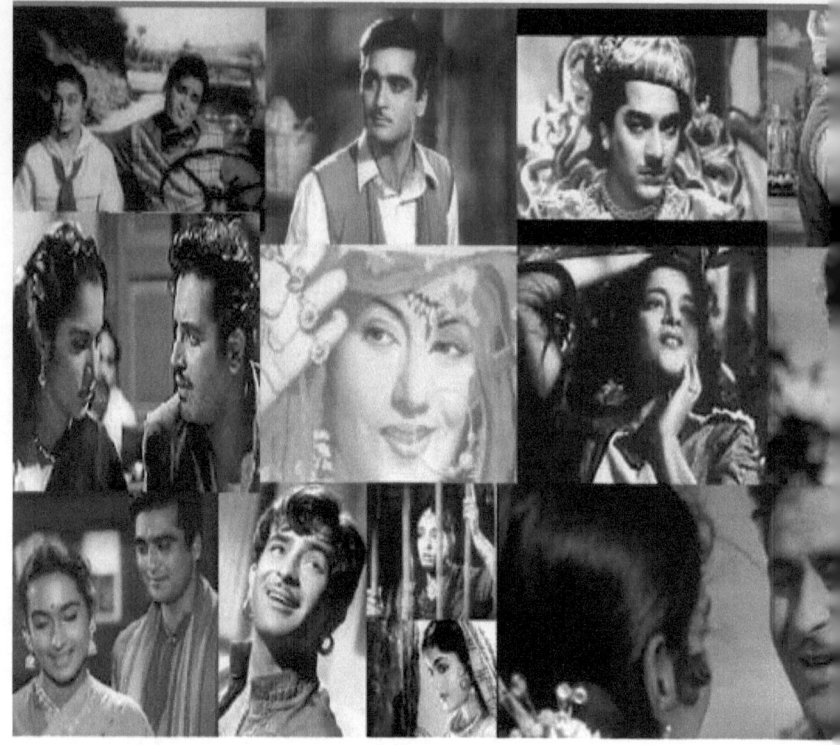

Indian cinema has an identity that is very unique and unmatched. We have moved from the black and white silent films to 3D, but our cinema continues to retain its basic essence - to thrill. Even as internet downloads and television continue to cannibalize the theatrical revenues of Indian films, the lure of the 35 mm is something else altogether. It was Phalke who introduced India to world cinema at a time when working in films was taboo. After the success of his film 'Raja Harishchandra', several filmmakers in Bombay and Madras began making silent films. By the mid 1920s, Madras had become the epicentre for all film related activities. Raghupathi Venkaiah Naidu, SS

Vasan, AV Meiyappan set up production houses in Madras to shoot Telugu and Tamil films.

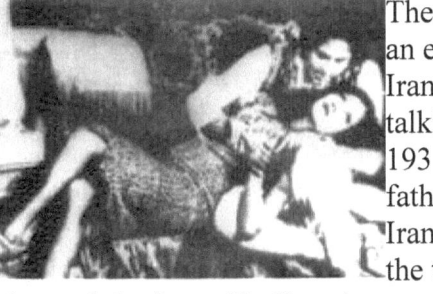The silent era came to an end when Ardeshir Irani produced his first talkie, 'Alam Ara' in 1931. If Phalke was the father of Indian cinema, Irani was the father of the talkie. The talkies changed the face of Indian cinema. Apart from looks, the actors not only needed a commanding voice but also singing skills, as music became a defining element in Indian cinema. The year also marked the beginning of the Talkie era in South Indian films. The first talkie films in Bengali (Jumai Shasthi), Telugu (Bhakta Prahlad) and Tamil (Kalidass) were released in the same year.

The forties was a tumultuous decade; the first half was ravaged by war and the second saw drastic political changes all over the world. In the middle of the Second World War in 1945 came 'Kismet' starring Ashok Kumar which became one of the biggest hits in the history of Indian cinema. It had some bold themes - the first anti-hero and an unmarried pregnancy. It clearly showed that the filmmakers of the era were bolder than the times in which they were living in. A close relationship between epic consciousness and the art of cinema was established. It was against this backdrop that filmmakers like V.Shantaram, Bimal Roy, Raj Kapoor and Mehboob Khan made their films. In the meantime, the film industry had made rapid strides in the South, where Tamil, Telugu and Kannada films were taking South India by storm. By the late 1940s, films were being made in various Indian languages with religion being the dominant theme. 1940s to late 1950s was also the golden era of music. Shankar Jaikishan, O.P. Nayyar, Madan Mohan, C. Ramchandra, Salil Chaudhury, Naushad, S.D. Burman - all had their distinctive style. Each vied with the other to produce some of the most unforgettable melodies India has ever known.

50s and 60s were considered as the Golden Age of Indian cinema. Filmmakers like Satyajit Ray, Ritwik Ghatak, Guru Dutt, Bimal Roy, Mehboob Khan, K Asif, Raj Kapoor, KV Reddy, L V Prasad and Ramu Kariat made waves in their respective film industries and they went on to make classics like Pather Panchali, Madhumati, Do Bheega Zameen, Shree 420, Awaara, Pyasa, Mother India, Mughal E Azam, Mayabazar and Chemmeen among many other films. In the south, N.T. Rama Rao, M. G. Ramachandran, Sivaji Ganesan, Rajkumar, Prem Nazir dominated the film industry for more than three decades before making way for the next generation of actors like Rajinikanth, Kamal Haasan, Mammootty, Mohanlal, Chiranjeevi and Balakrishna.

The 70s completely changed the way films were made, especially in Hindi film industry. Changing social norms and changing economies influenced movies and the companies that made them. The narrative style changed. The story structure changed. Characters changed. Content changed. Masala films were the demand of the time. The genre promised instant attraction and had great entertainment value. It was the age of the angry young man and Amitabh Bachchan rose to prominence thanks to the success of Sholay,

Zanjeer and Deewar. While Dev Anand, Rajesh Khanna, Jitendra and Dharmendra continued to bask in the glory of back to back hits, the actresses were not far behind. Right from the time of Savitri, Vyjayanthi Mala, Nargis, Waheeda Rahman and Sharmila Tagore to Sridevi, Rekha, Smita Patil, Hema Malini, several actresses became heartthrobs of the nation.

While Indian commercial cinema enjoyed popularity among movie-goers, Indian art cinema did not go unnoticed. Adoor Gopalakrishnan, Ritwik Ghatak, Aravindan, Satyajit Ray, Shyam Benegal, Shaji Karun and several other art film directors were making movies that gave India international fame and glory.

The eighties saw the advent of women film makers such as Vijaya Mehta ('Rao Saheb'), Aparna Sen ('36-Chouwringhee Lane', 'Parama'), Sai Pranjpye ('Chashme Baddoor', 'Katha', 'Sparsh'), Kalpana Lajimi ('Ek Pal'), Prema Karanth ('Phaniamma') and Meera Nair ('Salaam Bombay'). It was also the decade when sultry siren Rekha wooed audiences with her stunning performance in 'Umrao Jaan' in 1981.

And then in 90's, it was a mixed genre of romantic, thrillers, action and comedy films. A stark upgrade can be seen on the canvas as technology gifted the industry Dolby digital sound effects, advanced special effects, choreography and international appeal. The development brought about investments from the corporate sector along with finer scripts and performances. It was time to shift focus to aesthetic appeal. And stars like Shah Rukh Khan, Rajnikanth, Madhuri Dixit, Salman Khan, Aamir Khan, Chiranjeevi, Juhi Chawla and Hrithik Roshan began to explore ways to use new techniques to enrich Indian cinema with their performances.

In recent years, Hindi cinema has undergone a massive change due to the emergence of new age filmmakers like Anurag Kashyap, Rajkumar Hirani, Dibakar Banerjee and Vishal Bhardwaj. Of late, Tamil and Marathi cinema has witnessed similar changes with several new filmmakers coming forth to cater to a niche audience.

As the world has become a global village, the Indian film industry has reached out further to international audiences. Apart from regular screenings at major international film festivals, the overseas market contributes a sizeable chunk to Bollywood's box office collections. Regular foreign Investments made by major global studios such as 20th Century Fox, Sony Pictures, and Warner Bros put a stamp of confirmation that Bollywood has etched itself on the global podium.

How Bombay became Bollywood - the silent era
A lot has changed since the time the the first feature film, 'Raja Harishchandra' was released in Mumbai in 1913. Music, drama, powerful dialogues have become an integral part of cinema and has even permeated into our lives. The grandeur, the aplomb that we associate cinema to in present times is a stark contrast from how cinema was when it was initially introduced. As Indian cinema turns 100 years this year, we look at the initial phase of

Indian films- silent films which gave emphasis to images and treated them as canvases.

Like most things in India, the origins and history of cinema in India is quite fascinating. Fascinating - because the origins of cinema started sometime in 1890s and not 1913 as it is popularly known now. Also, if one looks back, one can understand how the society and certain situations influenced the way the film industry works now - 100 years down the line.

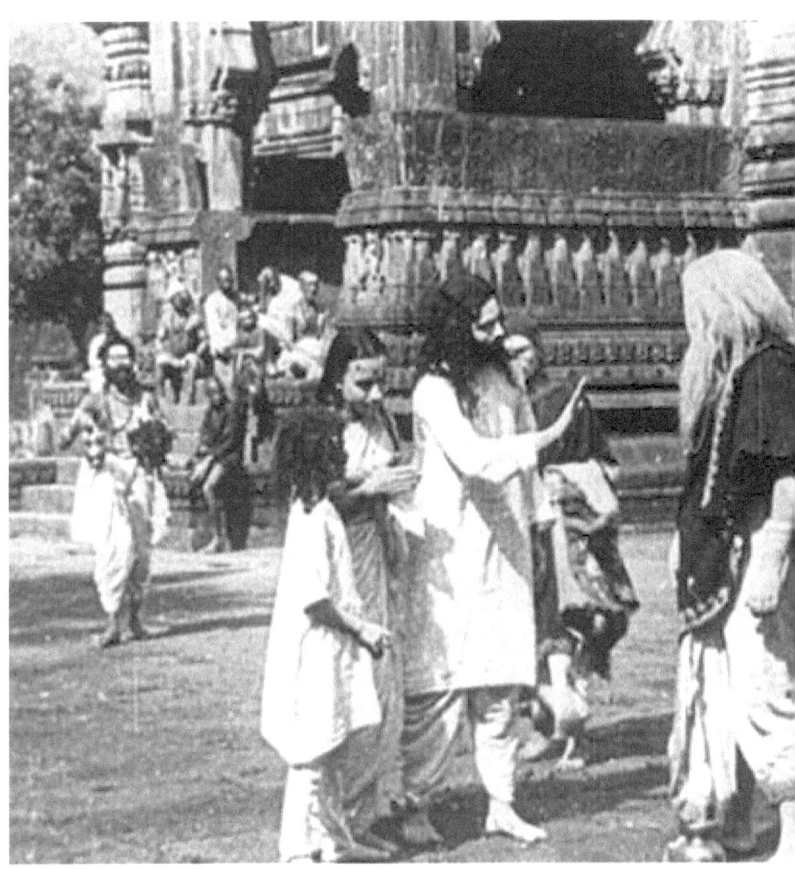

Dada Saheb Phalke's second film 'Lanka Dahan' (1917) was based on Ramayan and went on to become India's first box office hit.

The year was 1896 and Frenchmen - the Luemiere brothers came down to Bombay to showcase short films. For the European population as well as the Indians who were present at the screening, the concept of moving images was simply fascinating. Till then, photography was a known medium but films were still new. A year later, short films were also screened at the Victoria Public Hall in Madras by an European exhibitor.

Most of us know that Dadasaheb Phalke heralded feature films in India, but contrary to popular notions, he wasn't the first to make a silent film. HS Bhatavdekar popularly known as Save Dada, a photographer by profession was one the privileged few to have witnessed the films made by Luemiere brothers in 1896. Soon after, Bhatavdekar procured a movie camera from London and went on to document day-to-day events which eventually made for India's first silent short film in 1897.

The origins of India's three most prominent film industries can be traced to these years when European exhibitors showcased foreign films in Bombay (1896), Madras (1897) and Calcutta (1898). All these cities played an important part in forming the subsequent Marathi, Tamil and Bengali film industry which till date are flourishing. Soon after Save Dada, photographer Hiralal Sen also made his first film, 'A Dancing Scene' from the opera 'The Flower of Persia'. Sen, subsequently started his film company, Royal Bioscope Company with his brother, Motilal and went on to make forty films in his career.

By the late 1890s, short films had become a common feature and many photographers had experimented with medium. Most of these films were documentaries capturing events and some captured theatrical performances.

1913-1931

Heavily influenced after watching 'The Life of Christ', photographer and printing press owner Dhundiraj Govind Phalke wondered why weren't there Indian films based on the Hindu Mythology. Phalke started filming 'Raja Harishchandra' in 1912 which was commercially released in Bombay in 1913 and thus India got its first feature film.

'Raja Harishchandra' also was the first silent film which was screened in Coronation Cinema in Mumbai for the public. Till then films that were being made were viewed by only certain section of the society.

The first film starred an actor called DD Dabke, who went on to remake 'Raja Harishchandra' again in 1924. As the society was a closed and conservative one, women were not allowed to act and male actors played female chacaters in the film. Having worked with Raja Ravi Verma, Phalke was deeply influenced by the painter's style and incorporated the same style in his debut film. The film narrated the story of the noble and righteous king, Harishchandra, who first sacrifices his kingdom, followed by his wife and eventually his children to honour his promise to the sage Vishwamitra.

Silent films in the South

Phalke's film heralded a new era. That of full length feature films. Around the same time, different filmmakers started experimenting with this new, fascinating medium and several silent films were made in various states. The Telugu film industry also made its foray into films in 1912 but the the film- 'Bhisma Pratighna' was released only in 1921. In Bengal, six years after 'Raja Harishchandra', Madan Theatre Company released its first silent film 'Billwamangal' in November 1919.

Most films stuck to mythology as its primary theme. Phalke's second film 'Lanka Dahan' (1917) was based on Ramayan and went on to become India's first box office hit. Films like Keechaka Vadham(1917), Shankuntala(1920), Bhakt Vidur (1921) were all based on mythology. Even though the films lacked diaoluges, the visual delight made the features captivating. The love stories that India films heavily bank upon now also had its origins in the silent era. The first love story was made by Dhiren Ganguly called 'Bilet Ferot' in 1921. By 1920s India was producing more than 27 films a year- a big number for that era.

Himanshu Rai

Himanshu Rai, who was a prominent filmmaker of the 1940s, also began his career by co-directing a silent film called 'Prem Sanyas' in 1925. Rai and Franz Osten shot the film in Lahore and Rai's wife Devika Rani played the lead role in the film.

By the late 1920s, filmmakers slowly started adapting novels for films and started steering away from mythology. Phalke produced and directed films till in the 1932 but eventually, as the talkies came into being, could not sustain himself in a changing industry and retired in Pune.

The first talkie

By the time the first talkie - Ardeshir Irani's 'Alam Ara' came in 1931, Indian audience was familiar with the concept of a feature film. Several theatres had been opened in various cities of the country and filmmakers were slowly introducing new stories. Irani perhaps understood the importance of sound in films and reportedly raced to finish the film. When the film was released in Mumbai's Majestic Cinema, the police had to be summoned to control the hysterical crowd who had come to watch the film.

While 'Alam Ara' brought a new change in the society it affected the careers of many filmmakers. Several pioneering filmmakers who were till then making silent films retired and faded into the oblivion with advent of the talkies as they could never cope with the changing times nor were they willing to understand the importance of sound in feature films.

Movies which talks about India

With the <u>Toronto International Film Festival </u>(TIFF) quickly approaching — and this year the Spotlight City is Mumbai — now seems like a good time to make a list of my top 10 favourite movies about India. These are not necessarily Indian-made movies — but movies that reveal the history and culture of the country. I have arranged them in chronological order of the time period they depict (not when they were made), so if you watch them in this order, you will get a sense of the history of India over the past couple of hundred years. Not too many "Bollywood films" on the list — but if you want to know more about the booming Hindi cinema industry in Bombay/Mumbai, read my <u>Bollywood Primer</u>.
NOTE: TIFF is not the only Canadian film festival honouring Indian films in the month of September. So is the Canadian Film Institute with the <u>9th Indian Film</u>

and the 13th Annual .

1. *Jodhaa Akbar*

Jodhaa Akbar is a big Bollywood blockbuster of a film; it swept all the awards the year it was released. It's about the relationship between India's Mughal Emperor Akbar, who was of course Muslim, and his Rajput-Hindu wife Jodhaaa. It stars the impossibly good looking on-screen couple Aishwarya Rai Bachchan and Hrithik Roshan. Jodhaa Akbar, set in the 16th century, is a sweeping historical saga dripping with romance, intrigue and absolutely fabulous REAL jewelry. A very satisfying film experience.

WHAT YOU LEARN: India has been a diverse and sophisticated civilization for hundreds (if not thousands) of years.

2. *Lagaan*

Lagaan means "tax" — the tax paid by Indian subjects to their British overlords; and the film Lagaan, set during the Victorian era, is about a tax revolt by overburdened villagers. The tax revolt crisis leads to a cricket match challenge between the villagers, who have never played the game before — led by Aamir Khan, in the role that propelled him to stardom — and the British. It's a feel-good movie on a grand scale about national pride. Made by the same director as Jodhaa Akbar, Ashutosh Gowariker, but earlier in his career. It's great to watch post-colonial people taking pride in their culture and history, even if it means playing up stereotypes and formulaic plot lines. Aamir Khan is awesome. As usual. **WHAT YOU LEARN:** Cricket may have came from England, but India has taken it to heart.

3. Pather Panchali

Some people think its Orson Welles, some Stanley Kubrick, others Kurosawa. But I think Satyajit Ray, who hailed from Bengal in eastern India, is the greatest film director in the history of cinema and this "little" film (budget was purportedly $3,000) was his debut. Pather Panchali, which means "Song of the Little Road," is a study of rural family life in India in the early part of the 20th century. It is perhaps the most sensitive and true-to-life film I have ever seen. A lyrical masterpiece, and the first of the three Apu Trilogy films that also includes Aparajito and Apur Sansar.
WHAT YOU LEARN: Why Indians glorify traditional, pastoral life. And why Ray is lionized.

4. Water

Water is one of my all-time favourite films. When I saw it for the first time at TIFF the year it debuted, I cried my eyes out at the dramatic end. Directed by Indo-Canadian powerhouse Deepa Mehta, Water is about life in a widow's ashram in India in the 1930s. The freedom struggle, which was gathering steam at the time under the charismatic leadership of Mahatma Gandhi, provides the backdrop. It took Deepa Mehta years to make this film as her set was burned by Hindu fanatics. Eventually, she shot it in Sri Lanka. (Note to self: must find out where it was shot before I go to Sri Lanka in December!) **WHAT YOU LEARN**: Life for women in India is unfair; and when personal conscience triumphs societal beliefs, good things happen.

5. *Passage to India*

This is my favourite film about India! Based on the book by E.M. Forster, directed by David Lean and with an all-star cast that includes Victor Banerjee, Alec Guinness and Peggy Ashcroft, Passage to India is about the clash between the British colonizers and their Indian subjects in the years just before independence. The story centres on Judy Davis' character, Adela Quested, who "goes out to India" with her future mother-in-law, Mrs. Moore (Peggy Ashcroft) to be with her fiance, a British bureaucrat. I love the scene when Mrs. Moore meets Dr. Aziz in the mosque; it has haunted me for many years; and I recall studying the significance of the Marabar Caves in university, long before the film was made. The book, the story and the film has made an indelible impression on me.

WHAT YOU LEARN: The dynamics between Britishers and Indians, the oppressors and the oppressed, was complex. Plus, there are mysterious forces at work that can overturn any political or societal structure built by men.

6. Gandhi

Can't have a list of films about India without the epic <u>Gandhi</u> figuring prominently. Directed by David Attenborough and starring Ben Kingsley as Gandhi, it swept the Oscars in 1982. It's a historical, biographical, cultural epic and an acting tour de force. There's really no point in reviewing it; everyone has seen it; it's about the greatest figure of the 20th century (in my opinion) and one of the most incredible stories in history — and Ben Kingsley pulled it off. I love that scene when John Gielgud as Lord Irwin says, "You mean he wants us to just walk out of India?" Yes. Yes he does. And they did. Freeing 350 million people. Incredible.
WHAT YOU LEARN: Non-violent, passive resistance can be a very, very powerful weapon.

7. Earth

But … then the Partition of India happened. Earth was the second film in Deepa Mehta's elements trilogy (Fire, Earth and Water), and it's about what happens to a group of friends in Lahore when Partition divides their lives in half. At the centre of the friendship circle is Lenny, a little Parsi girl crippled by polio, and her ayah, who is a ravishingly beautiful young Hindu woman (Nandita Das). They go regularly to the park, where a group of men — Muslim, Hindu and Sikh — surround them in quiet appreciation of ayah's beauty. As August 15, 1947 and the independence of India approaches, Partition is announced: a line will be drawn through the populous state of Punjab to create Pakistan, and no one knows where the line will be, and whether Lahore will end up in secular India or Muslim Pakistan. Tensions start to erupt as the various religious-based factions form. Aamir Khan is excellent (as always) as the Ice-candy-man, an intense young Muslim man in love with ayah; and I fell in love with Rahul Khanna in this film, who played the sensitive masseuse who wins her love. The film was based on a book called Cracked India by Bapsi Sidhwa, which is superb.

WHAT YOU LEARN: The decision to rip India apart and separate brother from brother, and sister from sister, was brutal — and its force is still being felt.

8. Rang de Basanti

Jump ahead to modern India. A British woman whose grandfather was a police officer in India in the 1920s travels to Delhi to make a film based on his diaries and about his involvement with the famous freedom fighters Bhagat Singh, Chandrashekhar Azad (played by Aamir Khan) and their contemporaries. She meets a group of young people with no political convictions, but after she casts them in the documentary to play the freedom fighters, and one of their circle dies because of political corruption, they become activists. When I was in India the first time, in 2006, Rang de Basanti was a huge hit, and it galvanized a lot of young people to take action. In fact, they copied the candle-lit, India Gate sit-in from the film. With this film, you'll learn a lot about both the early days of the freedom struggle and modern-day India. **WHAT YOU LEARN:** Indians are very proud of their culture, their heroes, and the successful outcome of their struggle for independence.

9. *Slumdog Millionaire*

Directed by Danny Boyle, famous for Trainspotting and the London Olympics opening ceremonies. I walked into the theatre with an Indian friend and a skeptical attitude. But <u>Slumdog Millionaire</u> blew both my friend and I away. It's a tour de force. Though made by a "foreigner," this film really captures something truthful about the realities of life in modern-day India. Plus, it is entertaining, well-made, fast-paced and engaging. **WHAT YOU LEARN:** Life can brutal in the slums of India. But, like everywhere else, hope is a potent elixir.

10. *Delhi Belly*

This film answers the burning question, is there a Quentin Tarantino in India? Well, no. But if there was, it would be the people who made <u>Delhi Belly</u>. I like it a lot better than Tarantino, though, because it's way more fun and doesn't take itself seriously — you can read my review here, <u>Why Delhi Belly is a good thing</u>. This film is on the list because it's so "modern." It's not a "Bollywood" film and it's not serious — it's a dark comedy with lots of vulgarity and a completely implausible plot — but it does show a slice-of-life of modern, middle-class, creative professionals. In other words, people like me, but in Delhi. And running from murderous diamond smugglers.

WHAT YOU LEARN: Don't eat tandoori chicken from a filthy street vendor in Old Delhi.

11. Monsoon Wedding

The bonus film is by Mira Nair, a fantastic director who tackles social issues head on. (She also directed Salaam Bombay, which was set in the slums of Bombay/Mumbai.) Monsoon Wedding is about an upper-middle-class family preparing for a wedding and it's one of my favourite films (like Water, it features the music of my good friend, Canadian musician Mychael Danna). As someone who's been part of a big Punjabi family in Delhi, I can tell you from personal experience that this film is true to life, and does show what it's like on the "inside" of family life.

WHAT YOU LEARN: In India, family is everything.

History of the kiss - sexually liberated 1930s to prudish 21st century

For almost four decades, Bollywood's only association with intimacy was two nodding dandelions and the camera panning to logs burning in the fireplace. Desire was portrayed through symbolism on the celluloid as filmmakers learned to fear the censor board. But this wasn't always the case in cinema's 100 year history. Actresses were as bold in the 1930s as they are today, perhaps even more.

But interestingly, only a few know that Bollywood was the boldest during its nascent stage. In the early 1920s and 30s, kissing was a common phenomenon. With Indian film industry entering its 100th year, we take a look at good, bold cinema in early years of Bollywood and how later it disappeared from the celluloid in the 1950s only to return in the late 70s.

It was in the late 80s that the filmmakers began to show content that challenged the conservative nature of the censor board.

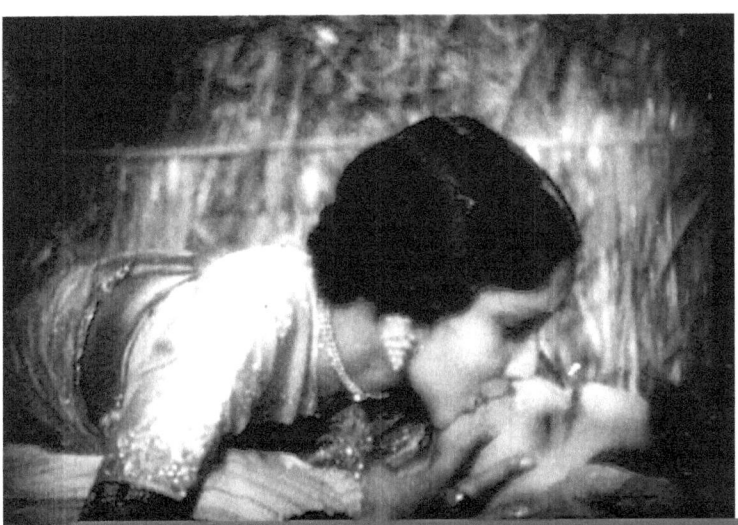

Actresses were as bold in the 1930s as they are today, perhaps even more.

The bold heroines of the silent era

With influence of English cinema and joint ventures with foreign production houses, the early films had a liberal dose of sex and kissing scenes. Unlike the actresses of 60s and 70s, the heroines of early 20s and 30s did not shy away from on-screen intimacy. There was a four-minute kiss between Devika Rani and her director husband in the 1933 film "Karma', but it was actually Seeta Devi who was the first actress to lock lips on the silver screen.
In her 1929 silent film 'A Throw of Dice', Seeta Devi went on to kiss Charu Roy. Based on Mahabharata, the

film is about two kings who are vying for the love of a hermit's daughter.

Another popular actress of those times, Zubeida, created a sensation back in 1932 with her scanty attire and kissing scenes in film 'Zarina'. Even Lalita Pawar, who later became popular in Bollywood for playing the vamp, had a kissing scene in 'Pati Bhakti' in 1920s.

These actresses broke new ground in the male-dominated film industry. They moved away from the shackles of conservatism and carved a path for themselves during the initial days of Bollywood.

Censorship in late 1940s

Till the mid 40s, Hindi films freely used bold content but with independence from British rule in 1947 and the establishment of the Film Advisory Board, the industry became more conservative. With the new found freedom, the Board wanted the filmmakers to present India in its chaste form. And most of celluloid's sensuality was made obsolete following the formation of the Cinematograph Act 1952. The Act had put a hold on kissing on-screen by calling it 'indecent'. Bollywood became discreet in showing any overt display of affection.

Symbolism takes over in 1950s-60s

With every frame of the film being scrutinized by the censor board, the filmmakers developed their own ways of portraying romance on the silver screen. If kissing and love making scenes were banned from the celluloid, the filmmakers showed intimacy on screen through symbolism. While touching of hands and caressing of cheeks was acceptable on the screen, the filmmakers used two flowers touching as the sign of kissing or coitus between couples. In the 50s and 60s, running around trees replaced kissing.

Filmmakers used fire as a symbol for desire and the popular 'Roop Tera Mastana' song from the 1969 film 'Aaradhna' showed the camera panning to burning logs to hint at lovemaking.

Boldness knocks on screen in 1970s-80s

The films of the 1950s and 60s were high on romance but the censor board prompted by a conservative society marred the creative freedom of the filmmakers. But with the dawn of 1970s, the filmmakers decided to keep up with the changing society. Director Raj Kapoor never ceased from displaying a certain sense of sexuality in his films. He either titillated the audiences by making his actresses wear a swimsuit or would show them in wet saris.

Raj Kapoor reprised the trend of kissing on screen with his 1973 film 'Bobby'. In a teenage romance drama, the director did not just make the actress wear the skimpiest of the clothes, but he also encouraged Rishi Kapoor and Dimple Kapadia to kiss on screen. Kapoor yet again made Shashi Kapoor and Zeenat Amam lock lips in the 1978 film 'Satyam Shivam Sundaram' later in the decade. He later took boldness to a new level with his film 'Ram Teri Ganga Maili'. Mandakini sitting under a waterfall, with her breasts clearly outlined through her wet saree became the most-talked-about scene in the film.

Keeping with the new found freedom on-screen, the other filmmakers also followed in his footsteps. Dimple

Kapadia became the new symbol of sexual liberation in the mid-80s when she kissed Rishi Kapoor in the 1985 film 'Sagar' and later her steamy romance with Anil Kapoor on-screen in 'Janbaaz' became the talk of the town.

Dancing diva Madhuri Dixit also kissed Vinod Khanna in the 1988 film 'Dayavan'. Even new kids on the block in late 1980s, Juhi Chawla and Aamir Khan shared a kiss on screen in 'Qayamat Se Qayamat Tak'.

Bold gets bolder in 1990s -2010

With the advent of 1990s, kissing became a common phenomenon on the celluloid. But, it was Karisma Kapoor and Aamir Khan's minute long kiss in the 1996 film 'Raja Hindustani' that created a stir.

Taking a cue from their predecessors, the new filmmakers took boldness to a new level on-screen. In 2003 film 'Khwahish', Govind Menon made Mallika Sherawat and Himanshu Malik kiss 17 times on screen. The film was a flop at the box-office but it did get much publicity. Later many directors chose to touch on the subject of lust as an easy ticket to the box office. Neha Dhupia's 2004 film 'Julie' bombed at the box office despite her claims that sex sells in Bollywood.

But it was Anurag Basu's erotic thriller 'Murder' that created a stir in Bollywood. Emraan Hashmi and Mallika Sherawat became overnight stars with their sexual chemistry in the film. Later actors like Hrithik Roshan and Aishwarya Rai followed their footsteps in 'Dhoom 2' and Shahid Kapoor and Kareena Kapoor in 'Jab We Met' and Vidya Balan and Arshad Warsi in 'Ishiqiya'.

100 Years of Indian Cinema: Homosexuals and the third gender on celluloid

When sexual revolution swept through the West in the 1960s after the advent of the birth control pill, some of the effects of the change found slanted reflections in popular culture. But for the ripples to hit the Indian shores, where cinema was still bound by Victorian puritanism, it took another decade. In all of cinema's history, true representation of alternate sexuality happened only as recently as the 70s driven by the worldwide gay rights movement.

While Hollywood cast Bobby Watson as a gay fashion designer named Paisley as early as 1931 in the film 'Manhattan Parade' and Marlene Dietrich kissed a young woman on the lips in 'Morocco' (1930) , Indian films waited another 40 years to even hint at homosexuality. The mythologies of the nascent era of Indian cinema were gradually giving way to the more realistic family themes of the 40s and then the romantic genre of the 50s. While filmmakers were trying to step outside the beaten track of traditional Indian themes, there was no allowance for portrayal of same sex, a subject that was still taboo in a country where the discourse on sex itself is bound by moral restriction.

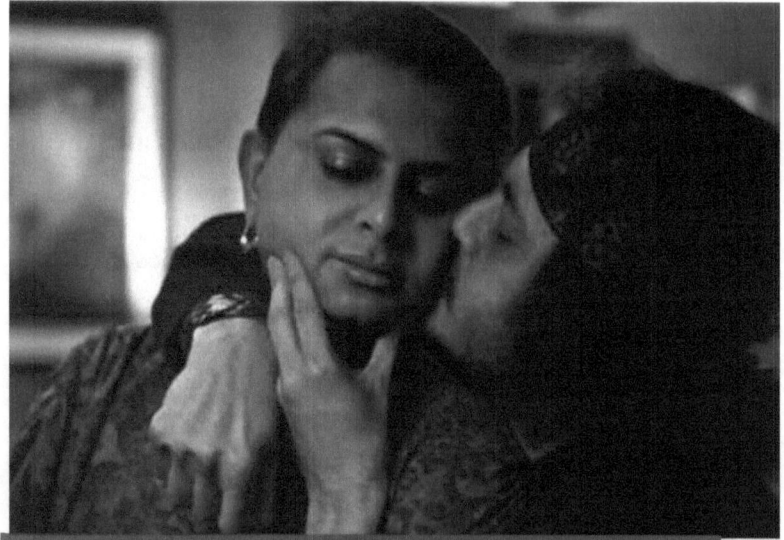

As we celebrate 100 years of cinema, we go back in time to see how the pioneers treated homosexuality on celluloid.

There's much archival evidence on the role cinema played in the last 100 years to break taboos and create tolerance towards the transsexuals, transgenders and homosexuals, though it has itself been guilty of perpetuating the worst stereotypes of sexual minorities for cheap laughs.

The third gender

The third gender played a significant role in Indian cinema, mainly in the form of eunuchs who invaded homes of women who have given birth to a male son. But very few serious films tried to focus on the conflicts and politics of their colonised living.

Santhosh Sowparnika's 'Ardhanari', Santosh Sivan's 'Navarasa' and David Atkins' 'Queens! Destiny of Dance' were seen as some later attempts to finally take the 'hijda' community seriously although they started to appear on celluloid in the late 70s in films such as 'Amar Akbar Antony'. The 90s filmmakers were more generous in awarding screen time to some notable third genders in films such as Mahesh Bhatt's 'Tamanna', setting a trend for films of the turn of the century - there were a whole bunch of them - Tamil film Appu (2000), Shabnam Mausi (2005), Shyam Benegal's 'Welcome to Sajjanpur' (2008) and Marathi film 'Jogwa' (2009) among others. For the first time, there was a concerted effort to empathise with the plight of the 'hijdas' beyond their exploitation in mainstream cinema for comic relief and painting them as a secretive, criminal community of degenerating moral and social system.

In the early years, when the leading men, be it Pramathesh Barua, Kundan Lal Saigal or MG Ramachandran, were still trying to find an identity in an industry that was in an experimental stage, the mannerisms on celluloid were direct extensions of the stage. The nasal dialogue delivery was not considered unusual for a time when cinema was yet to be influenced heavily by the roguish men of American westerns. This was also the time that the definition of the 'effeminate' underwent a sea change.

Foppish heroes of the 60s and 70s mirrored the fashion of their time and wore their hair in a coiffeur and pants hugging their waists. The method of self expression was urbane and distinct. It wasn't unnatural for men to shy away from bloodshed and heavy action till Amitabh Bachchan made grunge the look of the century in an explosive series of films that also cast a death blow to the last of the genteel heroes.

But filmmakers moved on from imparting a certain genteel charm to heroes who wouldn't get their hands dirty to introducing sissies - characters that contrasted with the macho gravity of the hero - for comic relief.

Queer identity

In the last twenty years the queer identity has come to be taken more seriously in arts. Books had men declaring their sexual identity in no uncertain terms while cinema struggled to strike a balance between the morally acceptable lines the makers still complied to with the changing times.

But films nevertheless shied away from any serious reference to homosexuality. Many consider a man's love for a clearly androgynous Paintal dressed as a woman in 'Rafoo Chakkar' (1975) to be cinema's first reference to homosexuality. The lines defining genders get blurred and the spurned lover accepts that 'no one's perfect' in a sexual insight amazingly cynical for its time in the climax.

Since then there have been parallel work in Malayalam, Bengali and Marathi cinema on same sex love. The 1982 Marathi film 'Umbartha' hinted at a lesbian relationship between two inmates of a remand home.

Pratibha Parmar made 'Flesh and Paper' (1990), a short on Indian lesbian poet Suniti Namjoshi. Deepa Metha's Fire (1998) was years late in coming in highlighting the struggles of lonely women trapped in unhappy marriages and bound by convention. But it still stirred up a hornet's nest in a country where sexual equality was a concept unheard of.

Ligy J Pullappally's Malayalam film 'Sancharram' (2004) beautifully portrayed the dilemma of two village belles embracing their sexuality. The 'Kamasutra' was of course the reliable handbook of sex that director Mira Nair adapted to a film in 1996 that celebrated intimacy between women. Buddhadev Dasgupta's Bengali film 'Uttara' (2000), was nuanced with homoerotic themes in his signature non-narrative poetic style.

While the mainstream tried to make its peace with homosexuality, the documentary scene was miles ahead in vision and competition. Nishit Saran filmed 'Summer

In My Veins' in 1999 on a mother coming to terms with her son's sexuality.

Kaizad Gustad's 'Bombay Boys' (1998) and Riyad Vinci Wadia's 'Bomgay' were the breakout films of this time to openly discuss homosexuality in the context of urban living.

Dev Benegal was filming 'Split Wide Open' with Rahul Bose and Laila Rouass, another significant narrative on homosexuality, probably at a time Ian Iqbal Rashid was finishing 'Surviving Sabu' - a film about a father and his gay son's

abrasive equation while working on a film project.

At a time when sexual rights were not even discussed in public, actress Rohini Hattangadi played a lesbian lover in Vijay Tendulkar's Marathi film 'Mitrachi Goshta' (1981).

In the south

The earliest references to gay theme in Malayalam cinema was 'Randu Penkuttikal' in 1978. Based on a story by Nanda Kumar, director Mohan narrated the obsessive love of a woman for a danseuse. There are homoerotic references in 'Deshadanakkili Karayaarilla' (1986) and the more recent and famous 'Sanchaaram' (2004), in Rithu (2009) and 'Paranja Katha' (2010).

In Tamil film 'Vettaiyaadu Vilayaadu' (2006), two men molested inside a prison by a gang of hijdas take on a life of crime. In the relatively conservative Tamil creative medium, director Venkat Prabhu managed to slip in a gay character in his film 'Goa'.

The shadow of invisibility

Cinema is undoubtedly the greatest thing to have happened to the queer movement in India. Doubted, ridiculed and criminalized for centuries, the sexual minorities stepped out from the shadow of invisibility after 2000 to claim their rightful place in popular culture. What followed was a plethora of films that were finally sympathetic to their plight.

Meant perhaps to free them from the shackles of strict convention, Madhur Bhandarkar's 'Page 3' (2005), Anurag Basu's 'Life in a... Metro' (2007), Reema Kagti's 'Honeymoon Travels' (2007), Karan Razdan's 'Girlfriend' (2004) and Parvati Balagopalan's 'Rules - Pyar Ka Superhit Formula' (2003) propagated the same gay stereotypes the filmmakers were trying to avoid. The mainstream has largely let down queer cinema.

But a whole host of films - shorts, documentaries and features - around this time were trying to understand the cultural phenomena of the queer movement. Few among those were 'Tedhi Lakeer' (2004), 'Teen Deewarein' (2003), 'My Brother Nikhil', Marathi film 'Thang' (2006), 'Touch of Pink' (2004), 'Stag' (2001), Water (2005), Yours Emotionally (2006), 'Piku Bhalo Aachhey' (Bengali, 2004), 'Happy Hookers' (2006), 'I Can't Think Straight' (2007) and 'Luck by Chance' (2009).

Special hat tip to Sridhar Rangayan, Onir, Rituparno Ghosh

In this context, the contributions of gay rights activists and filmmakers Sridhar Rangayan, Onir and Rituparno Ghosh to the genre have been immense. Rangayan, the assistant director of 'English, August' has made successive films in this genre - 'The Pink Mirror' (2006), 'Yours Emotionally' (2007) and '68 Pages' (2007).

Onir's 'I AM', an anthology film consisting of four short stories, won the National Award for Best Hindi Film and Best Lyrics.

If Sanjoy Nag's 'Memories of March' (2010) was a beautiful story of reconciliation starring Rituparno Ghosh, the latter's 'Chitrangada' (2012) remained restlessly dissatisfied in the search of sexuality. Kaushik Ganguly's Bengali film 'Aarekti Premer Galpo' about a gay director's obsession for his bisexual cinematographer was lauded at international festivals.

Bollywood

Meanwhile mainstream Bollywood tried in its own way to reconcile to the gay theme. But unfortunately the characterisations, even after all these years remained a spoof of a serious subject matter.

Films such as 'Dostana' and more recently 'Student of The Year' tried to introduce homosexuality in the plot but failed to create any commiseration due to the stereotypical spoofing of gay men. While a small section is still attempting to break the ice, it remains the job of a much larger and influential section of the cinema industry to push for reforms and overhaul the writing to bring out sensitive LGBT stories.

Parallel cinema – How art cinema is trying to sustain in modern era?

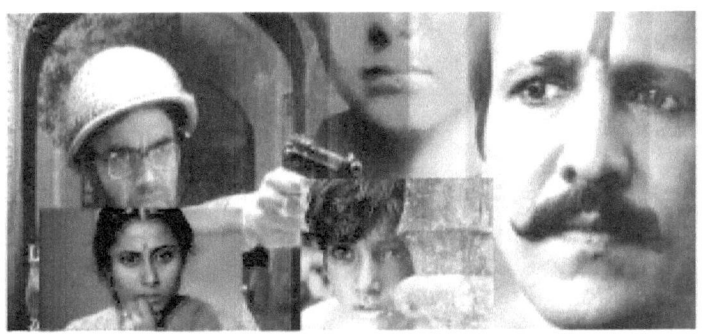

Movies have always been the most popular mode of entertainment in India. Every Friday there is buzz around cinema halls on a new release. According to the **Central Film Board of India** there were 1,288 feature films made in India in 2009 and 1,274 in 2010 but the number of art cinema films or better known as parallel **cinema** are still untraceable.

Parallel cinema known for its serious content, realism and depiction of social issues started in India way back in 1925 with **V.Shantaram's** 1925 silent film classic 'Savkari Pash' as one of the earliest examples. The movement, initially led by Bengali cinema, began to take shape from the 1940s to 1960s – a period often referred to as the 'Golden Age of Indian Cinema.' Most films made during this period were funded by the State Governments with an aim of showcasing an authentic **art** genre.

In the 70s and 80s era the art cinema started widening its wings in Hindi cinema as well Shyam Benegal, Gulzar, Mahesh Bhatt the directors of this era, tried their hand at promoting realism in their own different styles while embracing certain conventions of popular cinema in some of their other ventures. Slowly in the 90s parallel cinema saw its decline phase, the Bollywood got dominated with typical melodrama embraces fight, dance and songs.

Although parallel cinema has the power to drive change in society, throwing light on the harsh reality of society has been the main aim of this genre but as mentioned above, the charm of drama, item numbers and fight cannot be pulled out from Indian audiences and thus it gave birth to new form of cinema which included social issues with **Bollywood masala**.

Movies like **Dor, Gulaal, Udaan, Gangs of Wasseypur** deal with some of the critical social issues but they have also included the entertainment factor which audiences demand. Today there is a vast difference between old and new parallel cinema. Directors Satyajt Ray, Bimal Roy and Guru Dutt started together a wave in Indian Cinema marked as the 'Golden Period'. Now there are a few Indian directors trying to make impact. The current off-beat films, unlike the old parallel cinema, are less political and have little potential to create social impact. Due to more emphasis on business, movies are getting dominated by the commercial factor leading to fading point of parallel cinema.

Though there are some movies which have not compromised their content according to today's scenario such as '**The Ship of Theseus**' but at the end it is considered as an exceptional case. The question remains whether we are forgetting the essence of parallel cinema because of the influence of commercial factor in movies or whether we should blame ourselves for not appreciating the art cinema as a viewer?

INDIAN PARALLEL CINEMA

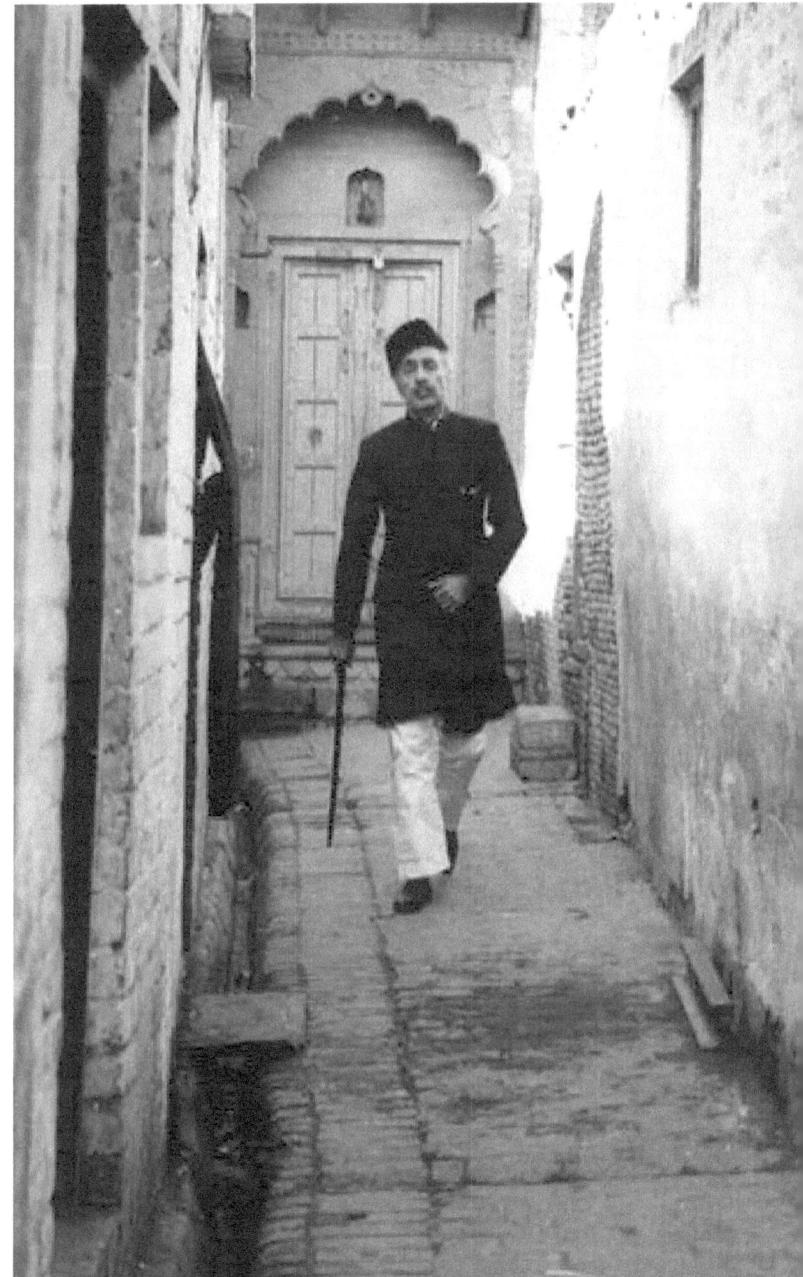

This is an attempt to catalogue the films of the parallel cinema movement. Most academics and scholars are in agreement that 1969 is probably an accurate starting point in terms of pin pointing the beginnings of parallel cinema with Mrinal Sen's FDC financed *Bhuvan Shome*. However, the end of the movement is far more problematic to isolate as the NFDC (National Film Development Corporation) continues to support indigenous and emerging film makers in terms of financial support. Though key film makers of the parallel cinema movement including Mrinal Sen are no longer active, exceptions exist in the form of Shyam Benegal.

With a low budget, no stars and the absence of any songs, *Ankur* (1973) truly was an unconventional Indian film. Benegal's social critique even bypassed the newly established FFC for funding, finding an unlikely partner in Blaze, an advertising company with which the director had close ties. With direct access to cinema exhibition across India, Blaze Films was established as an independent production company and distributor. Benegal says he was the one who approached Blaze with the idea of directing a feature film and their willingness to act as both producer and distributor was critical in breaking the monopoly of mainstream Hindi cinema by rejecting many of the established rules and helping to popularise the art house film as a commercially viable movement. Academic Madhava Prasad underlines the political relevance of Blaze as an independent distributor, '*Sensing the existence of a market for a cinema different from the popular as well as the 'middle class' variety, [Blaze] engaged one of its ad-film makers, Shyam Benegal to direct Ankur, thus inaugurating the commercial exploitation of the political dimension of the FFC's aesthetic project.'* (Prasad, 1998: 130)

With the unexpected commercial success of a film like *Bhuvan Shome* which performed tremendously well for a low budget art film, Blaze sensed that the emergence of a middle class audience versed in the language of European cinema could potentially evolve into a lucrative niche market. This hunger for the art film was qualified in the success of *Ankur*, cementing the development of a parallel cinema with which both Benegal and Shabana Azmi would become synonymous icons. However, the conditions for a new realist cinema spearheaded by Benegal were in no way a sudden phenomenon. The core argument for an alternative mode of cinematic address had originally been touted by the IPTA, a leftist theatre organisation that found many of its members actively involved in using film as an ideological instrument. However, the state's subservience to Hollywood imports and a reluctance to heed the advice outlined in a 1951 report by the S.K Patil Film Inquiry Committee delayed the inevitable emergence of an indigenous parallel cinema. Ashish Rajadhyaksha (1994: 25) says the 1951 report highlighted *'the shift from studio system to independent entrepreneurship'* whilst also recommending *'major state investment for film production, the setting up of a film finance corporation, a film institute and archives.'*

The monopolisation of the distribution and exhibition network by the major film making hub in Bombay would have definitely had an influence on why exactly the report was ignored as the recommendation for state investment would have raised concerns amongst many of the major producers who were not willing to share a market in which certain films would have favourable support from the government. State sponsored cinema even today tends to provoke a strong reaction amongst some directors who argue that such a situation in which the political values of the state and those of the film maker co exist is problematic in that the two will inevitably come to a consensus, thus diluting and compromising the ideological purity of the film's initial aims. Of course, this might be true of countries in which the ruling government does make use of ideological state apparatus like cinema as a means of circulating dominant values but the films that have been financed either partially or fully by the NFDC arguably share a leftist perspective that runs contrary to much of the conservative rhetoric espoused by consecutive Indian governments.

Taking just under ten years for the government to respond to the recommendations of the report, in 1960, the film finance corporation was established by Nehru with a remit that centred on supporting good quality films through financial assistance in the form of low interest loans. Admittedly, at first the FFC initially aligned themselves with established directors in the film industry, backing in particular Satyajit Ray. Rajadhyaksha argues that the commercial success of Bhuvan Shome was the turning point, encouraging the FFC to fully support 'low budget, independent films'. The acceleration of loans between 1969 and 1979 made to over fifty films launched the careers of numerous directors, leading to a vibrant and politically conscious cinema. Though the FFC continued to face a virtual embargo in terms of distribution and exhibition, Prasad (1998: 127-8) argues that *'the middle class movement in the mainstream industry was strong enough to prompt a suitable expansion of exhibition outlets'.* This was subsequently supported by opening the first FFC art house cinema in 1972 whilst *'in many cities, new theatres with reduced seating capacity were built specifically for the middle class film'.* (Prasad, 1998: 127-8) Simultaneously, the promotion of film culture through the emergence of film societies coincided with a new cine literate middle class audience.

Another equally significant factor often overlooked when contextualising parallel cinema is the decision taken by the government in 1971 to reject the renewal of a *'5 year contract for the import of Hollywood films.'* (Prasad, 1998: 190) The dislodging of Hollywood's domination was useful in opening up a new area of indigenous cinema as it meant Indian film makers no longer had to face the indignity of subservience. Even in light of today's American hegemony, India is one of the few nations in which the domestic box office each year is made up of home grown films. Ironically, it was Satyajit Ray who was the first to personally criticise the idea of a

New Indian Cinema arguing it was merely a pretentious euphemism connected with Godard and the French New Wave. Unlike Benegal and Nihalani who considered themselves 'middle of the road', the experimental and avant-garde cinema of European influenced Kumar Shahani and Mani Kaul represented the fringes of what had evolved into a rich national cinema. The drop in Hollywood imports inevitably led to a greater opportunity for indigenous films to negotiate with exhibitors. It was around this time in 1973 that Blaze released Benegal's debut *Ankur*, scoring an unexpected commercial success.

It was during the emergency declared by Indira Gandhi in 75 and onwards that the FFC faced its first real crisis. An investigation by The Committee on Public Undertakings in 1976 criticised the FFC for an art film bias and also failing to choose projects that stood a chance of turning a profit at the box office. As a direct consequence of the investigation, the FFC had to adopt a new *'aesthetic criteria for future film funding including human interest in theme, Indianness and characters with whom we can identify.'* (Rajadhyaksha, 1998) In 1980, the FFC merged with the Indian Motion Picture Export Corporation, becoming the NFDC (National Film Development Corporation). Two years later, the NFDC was involved in co-financing Richard Attenborough's biopic *Gandhi* (1982) and throughout the early 1980s, it experienced it's most instrumental and productive decade, distributing a catalogue of quality Indian films that have come to be regarded as the high point of parallel cinema. This period of prominence includes

award winning films such as *Aakrosh* (Cry of the Wounded, Govind Nihalani,
1980), *Anantram* (Monologue, Adoor Gopalakrishnan,
1987), *Ardh Satya* (Half Truth, Govind Nihalani,
1983), *Bhavni Bhavai*(A Folk Take, Ketan Mehta, 1980),
Chakra (Ravindra Dharmaraj, 1980), *Ghare-Baire* (The
Home and the Word, Satyajit Ray, 1984), *Jaane Bhi Do
Yaaro* (Who Pays the Piper, Kundan Shah,
1983), *Khandhar* (Mrinal Sen, 1983), *Salaam
Bombay* (Mira Nair, 1988), *Sati* (Aparna Sen, 1989)
and *Tarang* (Wages and Profit, Kumar Shahani, 1984).

It was in the nineties that Indian cinema started to change
yet again with both the family film and image of the
romantic hero revived in the films of new stars like
Shahrukh Khan and Salman Khan. Today, the NFDC
continues to support Indian art films and still finances a
number of films year each year. However, growth of
independent production companies, the rise in cinema
screens and the dominance of television have obscured
the role of the NFDC. Even the leading light of parallel
cinema Shyam Benegal turned to UTV Motion Pictures, a
newly established international production company, for
the production and distribution of his 2008 comedy
film*Welcome to Sajjanpur*. No equivalent art-film
movement as that of parallel cinema exists today but the
new wave of film makers including Ram Gopal Varma,
Vishal Bhardwaj and Anurag Kashyap certainly
acknowledge the realist aesthetic of auteurs like Benegal,
Nihalani and Shahani on their own work.

The Rise of Filmi-Bolly Music

The Talkie Era

The year 1931 not only marked the beginning of the "talkie" age, but it also naturally became the starting point for movie composers and singers. The playing field became instantly dominated by a handful of strong production studios most of which had their legacy firmly rooted in the silent era. Ardeshir Irani and R.S. Choudhury (Mehboob Khan's mentors) carried forward the Imperial Studios banner. Himansu Rai, the consummate English nobleman leveraged his experience with British and German moviemakers, Shantaram and Master Vinayak joined forces to further foster Prabhat Films, B.N. Sarkar moved his silent movie gear to South Calcutta where New Theatres was founded, Homi Wadia instituted Wadia Movietone, Sohrab Modi joined his mentors at Minerva, and Chandulal Shah deftly moved his Ranjit Studios banner into the age of sound. There were others like Madan Theatres (also Calcutta), but the names mentioned here would provide the bedrock foundation on which the future would grow and prosper.

The attitudes of that age were interesting. Capital was tight and only a handful of privileged and monied gentry could invest in movie studios. Most of them were carryovers from the silent era anyway. Movie-watchers were still the upper echelons of society. The production studio was the feudal lord. Employees of the company would not dream of quitting or moonlighting. And girls from "good families" would not even dream of having anything to do with the performing arts, least of all the cinema.

All that changed when two daring and beautiful young ladies broke the rules. Devika Rani Choudhury married Himansu Rai and stepped firmly in to moviedom. Not far away, a charming Durga Khote joined Shantaram's Prabhat Films in AYODHYECHA RAAJA, their first sound venture. These were still the exception to a rule deeply entrenched in a male-dominated tradition. But a beachhead was now created. Others would follow. Durga Khote can be credited with another first. She could well have been the first freelance heroine of that age. As committed as she was to Prabhat, she also spent some time working with the New Theatres contingent.

Musical tastes round the country were still dominated by the Indian motif - one-dimensional melody that drew almost entirely on classical and folk structures. The performance of music was simple at best. Most of the singers were either from "singing families" with delivery styles set in the tradition of their "gharaana" OR were theatre performers trying hard to get by with simple straight-line approximations of the stated melody. Playback technology was available, but there was no implementation handy for scalable reuse. Out in Bengal, New Theatres tried their first playback experiment as early as 1933. It did not go unnoticed.

This was the state of the early to mid '30s. The alliances were interesting. The East and West were ruled by their respective Holy Trinities. Prabhat was led by Master

Govindrao Tembe and his two disciples Keshavrao Bhole and Krishnarao Phulambrikar (with a young Vasant Shantaram Desai still in the pen). Bengal's New Theatres had their answer in Raichand Boral, Pankaj Mullick and later, Timirbaran Bhattacharya. Imperial Studios leaned on their Parsee patrons. Himansu Rai, with his British Production Company, was still dependent on European craftspersons for music among other things. Bombay Talkie, created in the mid-'30s would hire Khorshed Homji and Ramchandra Pal as their constant composers, but that was a few years away. Funded to a degree by Ram Daryani, Sagar and National Studios brought in maestros Pransukh Nayak and Ashok Ghosh. Chandulal Shah's Ranjit Studios flexed its musical muscle through classicists like Jhande Khan, Banne Khan and protege Rewashankar Marwari.

The somewhat negative perception of cinema's musical occupants, pervasive as it was, never quite influenced the classicists of any age, really. In the mid-'30s, grandmasters like Rabindranath Tagore and Kazi Nazrul Islam sought to use the movie medium to further the cause of literature, music, national integration, the independence movement, and on and on.

Emergence of Hindi movie song

And then it happened. Ram Daryani, a visionary financier, brought a 20 year old tabla player from Calcutta to work with the Sagar Movietone orchestra. It is to the credit of composer Ashok Ghosh that he took young Anil Biswas under his tutelage, and further, gave him enough freedom to create the first real orchestra for a Hindi movie song. In parallel, the Himansu Rai-Devika Rani team launched Bombay Talkie, hired the orchestra-minded Saraswati Devi as their composer, and further strengthened the foundation of a Western outlook, however simplistic it might have been at that time. The groundwork was launched for the Hindi movie song.

The first few songs to hit the nation as a whole may well have been from ACHHUT KANYAA and some contemporary Sagar Movietone productions. The time was 1935-36, and if this is where it started, we might have a candidate here for bringing in the Golden Age.

In the meantime, just out of the blue, New Theatres hit a home run. They augmented their singing talent through Sehgal's voice. A Punjabi singer far away from his native ambience seemed well at home in Tollygunge, South Calcutta.

With all the busy ins and out, Bombay had its weather eye cocked on an already well-established studio out to the North somewhere. Dalsukh Panchholi was an astute businessman. What did this business-oriented Lahori know of music, anyway? Some of life's happiest events hang together by threads of serendipity. Had Panchholi not created GUL-E-BAKAAVLI (1939), Baby Noorjehan may never have become known to the world at large. Had he not hired Master Ghulam Haider to do the very traditional, staid and Punjabi music for it, the songs may never have hit the headlines. And Panchholi might never have hired Master Haider to do KHAZAANCHI in 1941, but for a string of such chance events. And where would the Hindi movie song be today without the pioneering framework provided by KHAZAANCHI? We have fast-forwarded through the latter part of the '30s here, but let us get to 1941 and KHAZAANCHI. Master Haider consciously broke away from the dull and monotonous delivery of the '30s song. It was not without pain or criticism. Every generation has had its maverick. That he was, and knowingly so. KHAZAANCHI has gone down in history as the movie that defined the very structure of the modern Hindi song, much in the style of Von Neumann who, only 5 years later, defined the essence of stored program execution. Neither the structure of the Hindi song, nor the essential sequencial program execution model have changed much or at all since their inception. In that respect, Ghulam Haider hailed the age of modern Hindi music.

To summarize the '30s, the professional scene consisted of salaried employees in a handful of movie studios the vast majority of which were brought forward through profits from the silent age. Noorjehan, Ghulam Haider,and Anil Biswas were the frontline names. Looking at the content, we must examine the constituents - the melody, the orchestration, the singing style and ability, the lyrics, and in some ways also the picturization. The dominant singers of the age were KC Dey, Pankaj Mullick, Shanta Apte, Govindrao Tembe, Ashok Kumar, Devika Rani, Surendra, Wahidan Bai and sister Jyoti, Bibbo, Manju and a few more. In a category all by himself stood the theatrical and Sufiana singer

Kundanlal Sehgal. Some of his most famous songs had already been created, and he was just warming up.

More coincidence. The rapid and profitable emergence of the movie during the '30s, while remaining the sole property of a few studios, engaged the entire nation. What had started as the entertainment of the upper crust had trickled down to practically all layers of society - deep enough to threaten the legacy social outing. One such example was the Natak Mandali tradition of Maharashtra. Attendance dropped to all time lows. Mass defections occurred, both in the audience and the performers. Families whose wherewithal was the Natya Sangeet medium felt the most pain. Several went bankrupt. Alcoholism, a very natural companion of the performing arts, only aggravated the suffering. None knew this better than Dinanath Mangeshkar. Five children, a young wife, and nowhere to turn to. Once the darling of the Marathi stage, he now had trouble finding familiar faces in the business. In desperation, he accepted his oldest daughter's insistence upon finding a job for herself. In this quest, 12-year old Lata Mangeshkar was introduced to Vinayakrao Karnataki. But there was something else. She also signed up for a National Level Talent contest that had recently been labelled the KHAZAANCHI competition. The Northwestern frontier shuddered as the typhoon hit home. A Marathi-speaking winner of all things! Master Haider, the man whose runaway success had contributed the name to the contest, would stop to take notice. Seven years from the day, he would fight tooth and nail to permanently change the sound of Hindi music. Some milestone this. The writer must submit here that no matter when the Golden Era is said to begin, its life must include this landmark event of Lata Dinanath Mangeshkar winning the KHAZAANCHI competition. This voice has provided even our best composers with the motivation to produce the very best of melodies.

THE CULTURESPECIFIC USE OF SOUND IN INDIA CINEMA

PART I

The History of Sound in Indian Cinema

"The positive fallout of technological change will be a greater sensitivity among Indian audiences to sound in films; perhaps we may develop Indianness in sound in the way we use sound in Indian films, like our relationship with music."

Introduction :

Like everywhere in world cinema, sound in Indian cinema, has been marginalised to a fault. It is taken for granted as a part of the entire audiovisual ambience that cinema produces and reflects. Instead of being defined as having an independent, distinctive identity of its own, sound *per se,* has remained on the backburner, and everything associated with sound in Indian cinema has almost always, historically and in the present, been equated with music and song. Though music and song form an integral part of Indian cinema, there is no reason to ignore the contribution of sound *per se,* which of course, includes silence along with speech, voiceover, interior monologue, noise. In fact, the marginalisation of sound within the design of a film is obvious from the credit designation that is given to the sound engineer as 'director of audiography or, 'sound engineer' etc. though, in point of fact, the sound design of a film is as responsible for the quality of the final product as is the production design, the cinematography, the histrionics, the script and the direction. One never gets to see the phrase 'sound designer' in the credits of any film. In this scenario therefore, it becomes important to highlight the important role sound plays not only in contributing to the quality of a film, but also, and very significantly, the its role in cinema as a cultural signifier of a people. Critically speaking, very few film critics and reviewers pay attention to the use of sound and silence in their film critiques and reviews. Mainstream Indian cinema too, takes the sound design of an average film for granted, since songs and music form a major part of the narrative and cinematic space, and are almost automatic ingredients of Indian cinema.

The History of Sound:

The statistical story of the Indian sound film in its earliest years may briefly be summarised. It was, in large part, a story of new units, in which individuals from older companies were brought together by new capital. The Bombay producer who made the first talking feature, Alam Ara in the Hindi language was Ardeshir M Irani. Born in 1885, he started out in his family's musical instruments business, grown restless, gone into distribution of foreign films and finally, joined with tent showman Abdulally Esoofally in buying the Alexandra Cinema in 1914 and building the Majestic Cinema four years later.' Exhibition profits edged the partners into production. After involvement in several other companies, they launched the Imperial Film Company In 19262 and built a studio for it. In 1931 this company

won the sound race among Bombay producers. The equipment Irani obtained for the US was virtually 'junk' but somehow, via its singlesystem process, he completed *Alam Ara.* In this system, later used mainly for newsreels, sound goes directly onto the picture negative. In the more versatile double system, picture and sound are kept separate for flexibility in editing, to be combined in the laboratory as one of the final steps of the production process. Irani is said to have been strongly inspired by Universal's *Showboat* which he saw in New York. *Alam Ara* has never been described as an artistic triumph and no one seems to have preserved even a fragment of it. But its impact was astonishing. The Majestic theatre was besieged. Tickets disappeared into the black market. "Police aid had to be summoned to control the crowds .... Fouranna tickets were quoted ar Rs.4 and Rs.5.'" Later, units went on tour with the film, taking sound projection equipment with them, and everywhere drew surging crowds.

That same year, 22 other Hindi films appeared, and all seem to have made money. Also, in 193 1, three films in Bengali, one in Tamil, one in Telugu, appeared in their respective language areas. 1932 saw eight films in Marathi, two in Gujarati. In 1933, 75 Hindi features were made; production in other languages was also growing. Film after film appears to have had tumultous reception. Virtually all the films appear to have earned back their cost. In the 1930s, as one producer recalled wistfully, "almost all films made rnoney: By 1933, trepidation over the coming of sound had given way to unbounded optimism. That year, the compiler of *Who's Who in Indian Filmland,* in a jubilant preface gave expression to the mood:

What with scanty resources, stepmotherly Government aid, with keen competition from priviliged foreign films, with few technically qualified men, with no interested capitalists, with less interested fans, with actors and actresses scarcely able to spell their names (for it was thought a disgrace by society people to be associated with the screen), with no market excepting India, with censuring censors, with discouragement to the right, cheap sneers to the left, despair in front, and criticism from behind, the Indian Film Industry, thank God, has marched on and on to the field of victory, battling against a thousand other misfortunes. Has she not made a giant stride?

The reasons however, were not far to seek. Firstly , in a land where foreign languages dominated the councils and pleasures of the mighty for a thousand years, film in a vernacular tongue which the local man could understand, vested Indian cinema with a status it did not earlier enjoy. Secondly, sound granted the Indian producer 'natural protection.' He now had markets which foreign competitors would find difficult to penetrate. , the protection that the Government failed to give him through a quota system had now been conferred with the coming of the spoken word. But more than all this, there was another very strong potent at work. Songs.

Alam Ara included about a dozen songs. Another early Hindi film,*Indrasabha,* is said 4 to have had about around 59 songs. *Shirin Farhad* had 42 songs. An early Tamil film IS said to have had over 60 songs.' All the sound films produced in India in these early years had a profusion of songs. Most also had dances. Advertisements described some of these films as "all talking, all singing, all dancing" features. The Indian sound film, unlike the sound film of any other land, had from its first moment, seized*exclusively* on musicdrama forms. In so doing, the film had tapped a powerful current, one that had given it an extraordinary new impetus. It was a current that went back some 2000 years. In ancient India, in the Golden Age of Sanskrit theatre, the idea of drama was inseparably linked with song, dance and music. This has been the Indian tradition for many, many years, till 1000 A.D. when Sanskrit drama went into decline with the death of Kalidasa (ca.400 A.D.) It underwent a rebirth in the 19th century under

British rule. It flourished first in the form of private family theatres maintained in the large jointfamily homes of educated Indian families, specially in Calcutta.

Thus the sound film of 1931 was not only the heir of the silent film; it also inherited something more powerful and broadbased. Into the new medium came a river of music that had flown through unbroken millennia of dramatic tradition. While this strengthened the film, it also had other effects. It struck a mortal blow to rural and folk theatre performances in villages and smalltowns The sound film almost wiped out the reborn theatre with one brush of its hand. While cinema appropriated folk song and dance to its purposes, it changed these along the way. In their new environment, they began, quite naturally, to respond to new influences. The songs were ~formed through new instrumentation and new sometimes Western rhythms. Musicologists, just beginning to discover the same folk music, howled in anger at this sudden hybridisation and plagiarisation of traditional Indian tunes. Today this very 'hybridisation' defines the unique persona of Hindi film music and songs.

In 1931 and 1932, at what seemed a dark moment in Indian film history, song and dance in part derived from a tradition of folk musicdrama played an important role in winning for the sound film, an instant and widening acceptance. "With the coming of the talkies, the Indian motion picture came into its own as a definite and distinctive piece of creation. This was achieved by musical This same music was expected to temporarily block the Indian film from Western markets, and this proved to be a perceptive prophecy. It was also noted by observers that the obsession with music was a hazard to script values. The indiscriminate use of songs robbed the early talkies of narrative cohesion and dramatic force. Stories were loosely strung together to make room for songs and more songs.7 A film periodical commented: "Cases of singing before drawing a sword for a fight are not uncommon."' In the Indian film world, writers would have problems.

The First Sound Films:

In India, the earliest demonstration of what was known as 'Phonofilm' a process invented by Dr.Lee DeForest, in which sound was synchronised with the picture, was given at the Royal Opera House in Mumbai, in May 1927. The programme comprised of scenes from *Julius Caesar* with Basil Gill, the famous London actor, in the cast. Lillian Hall Davies and Miles Mander appeared in a comedy skit entitled *As We Lie.9*

The earliest attempts at synchronised sound film production in India were made by Madan Theatres. Early in 1929, Madan Theatres exhibited the first talking picture in India, Universal's *Melody of Love* at the Elphinstone Picture Palace in Calcutta. This was the first theatre in the East to be equipped with permanent sound apparatus. Soon after, on February 2 1, the same film was presented at the Excelsior Theatre in Mumbai By the end of 1930, more than 30 out of a total of 370 theatres in the country were technical ready for sound projections of film. 10 J.J.Madan had seen *The Jazz Singer* in New York. The tremendous public response to the film had convinced him about the unavoidable impact of sound in cinema.

Alam Ara is India's first fulllength sound film. It was released on l4th March, 1931 at Majestic Theatre, Mumbai (then, Bombay.) It narrowly beat *Shirin Farhad* (1931) to make cinema history. It established the use of music, song and dance as the mainstay of Indian cinema The film was a period fantasy based on Joseph David's popular Parsee theatre play and narrated a fairy tale. *Alam Ara* was made on the Tanar single system camera, recording image and sound simultaneously, which was difficult especially for the songs which were the film's highlights. Wazir Mobanurted Khan's rendering of a wandering minstrel's song number *de de khuda ke namme par pyaare was* particularly popular. It pioneered the use of a commentating chorus, a device adopted in several later films. In an interview with the Indian documentarist B.D.Garga, Irani said, "since there were no soundproof stages, we preferred to shoot indoors at night. Since our studio is located near a railway track... most of our shooting was done between hours that the trains ceased operation. We worked with a single system Tanar recording equipment...There were also no booms. Microphones had to be hidden in incredible places to keep out of camera range."" Along with his assistant Rustom Bharucha, he learnt the elementaries of sound recording from Wilford Denning, an American engineer, who had come to India to assemble the equipment for them. *"Alam Ara* shows the range and variety of sound reproduction involved in the production of a complete story ... it has shown that with due restraint and thouthfull direction, players like Vithal and Prithviraj and Miss Zubeida could by their significant acting and speech, evolve dramatic values to which the silent screw cannot possibly aspire. ,12

Within three weeks of *Alani Ara,* Madan Theatres released its first Bengali takie, *Jamai Shashthi.* This was followed with the release of *Shinn Farhad* in Hindi, also from the Madan's production house. This film beat *Alam Ara's*record at the box office. Three reasons given for its thumping success are : (a) the dialogue by Aga Hashar Kashmiri, (b) the songs sung by Kajan and Nissar and (c) the crystal clear recording done on the RCA Photophone. The recording for this film. was done on Double System Sound by foreign technicians. Madan Theatres turned out eight sound films in 1931 and 16 in 1932. Almost simultaneously with Hindi, films in different languages began to be made in the country. Among the first regional language films were *Jamai Sashti* in Bengali (193 *1), Kalidas* in Tamil (1931), *Bhakta Prahlad* in Telugu (1931), *Ayodhyecha Raja* in Marathi (1932), *Narsimha Mehta* in Gujarati (1932) and *Dhruva Kumar* in Kannada (1934.) But in terms of form and content, they were copies of the Hindi formula, full of songs, dances and music. The scenario has remained more or less the same today.

The Technique of Sound:

Technically speaking, during the earliest days of sound in Indian cinema, the Audio Carnex was the most popular among the sound recording machines used for filming sound. Around 1935, about 25 such machines were in use. Second in priority ranking was the Fildelytone, with 20 machines in operation. B.A.F. was in use in four studios. Other recording machines in use were Rico, Vinten, Visatone, R.C.A., Balsley and Phillips, Blue Seal, Adair Jenkins and Fearless." The Tanar Sound System was no longer in use by 1935 and two machines were lying idle in two studios. The introduction of sound changed the entire style of production and projection of motion pictures. It also led to the growth and adaptation of new equipment, and the creation of a hitherto unknown creative and technical vocation sound engineering. The first response to sound in cinema was to clarity of speech and song. If 80 per cent of the dialogue was clear and distinct, then producers were happy. 14 Earlier, when the cameras were noisy, their sound was controlled by using cotton blimps or cover. Silent cameras are a relative rarity in India. But a silent revolution has taken place in the technology of sound. Mani Kaul's Indian representation of Erotic *Tales* entitled *The Cloud Door* used Dolby SR for the transfer from negative to Beta video format to Avid (digitised computer system in which pictures and sounds are stored on hard disc) which is a nonlinear editing system, allowing for simultaneous editing of sound and picture. Avid offers the scope for non-destructive editing where original sound is not destroyed while cuttmg. The film was edited by Lalitha Krishna, exwife of Mani Katil, at Media Artists Studio in Chennai, considered to be the best in India. Sound processing in labs is now going through the process of being standardised. Sound labs are becoming conscious about the *quality* of sound rather than emphasise only clarity.

Sound technology in the country has shifted from optical to magnetic quite some time ago. Today, optical IS used only in the final stage of filmmaking. Magnetic technology offers greater range in sound than the mono-optical system. The earlier loop system of recording has made ay for the rocknroll system. New technology has made the hierarchy of sounds more complex, more exciting. Innovative sound designers like Vikram Joglekar and D. Wood have done a lot of experimenting with sound such as processing sound effects, bringing them close to music without necessarily musicalising it, sampling sound effects, taking reallife sound and arranging them in a certain way. Raja Dholakia who is a sound designer and music director, learnt to go beyond music to know, understand and apply the musicality of sound while working on the sound design of Mani Kaul's film*Siddheshwari,* an aesthetic impressionistic documentary on the famous thumri singer Siddheshwari Devi. "I tried to evoke the environmental influences in Siddheshwari's music through sounds" says Dholakia.

Masters of Sound among Indian filmmakers:

Some Indian filmmakers have paid close attention to the sound design of their films to combine aesthetics with realism in order to work out a smooth harmony between sound and other elements of film. Sadly, they are all from offmainstream cinema. Because, mainstream filmmakers have conveniently taken refuge under music, songs and longwinded dialogue, ignoring the significant of sound almost completely. The few mainstream filmmakers who need to be mentioned are Ramesh Sippy (Sholay), Dayal Nihalani *(Andha Yudh),* Mahesh Bhatt *(Saransh),* Partho Ghosh (Agni *Sakshi)* etc. B.R.Chopra, Subliash Ghai, Yash Chopra and Suraj Kumar BazJatya, who have broken several records at the box office with their stupendously successful films have worked out a strange blend of music and song to organise the entire sound design of their films. Their films spill over with songs and dances and with a lot of music on the soundtrack, sound effects*per se,* are cleverly sidetracked without hampering the aesthetics of the film. The characteristic sound effects associated with each entry of the dreaded dacoit Gabbar Singh in Ramesh Sippy's *Sholay* offers a model lesson on how sound can be used to signify the terror a character evokes. *Sholay is*also exemplary in its use of soundmatching to jump cut to a different scene and time, without breaking the continuity of the narrative, yet, intensifying the drama. Among offmainstream filmmakers Shyam Benegal picks up natural sounds despite the long footage of location shoots his films demand. He almost never uses the services of a dubbing theatre. GuIzar uses sound lyrically, since he is a poet himself and has a wonderful ear for music. Basu. Bhattacharya used sound as 'design by inference' which in common parlance, is known as the soundpicture counterpoint. In his film *Avishkar,* he uses the sound of a running train on the soundtrack to hint at the drifting apart of the couple who are in bed, like two passengers travelling towards the same destination, apparently together, but emotionally distanced. Kuar Shahani used a similar soundpicture counterpoint in *Tarang* whereas Govind Nihalani used it very strongly in the climactic scenes of *Party* and throughout the film in *Hazaar Chaurasi ki Maa.*

Hritwik Ghatak was a master of asynchronous and non-diegetic sound to produce irony and ambiguity in his films. In his essay, *Sound in Film"* he offers interesting examples of his own use of sound. In his *Meghe Dhaka Tara* (the Cloudcapped Star), he uses the sound of a whipleash while the camera closes in on the face of the heroine, the face registering an expression of deep, emotional pain, anguish, and helplessness. The impact is much more stronger and lasting than showing the woman crying would have been. "Sometimes, one has to comment on a particular piece of music in another director's film. I have done this myself In *La Dolce Vita,* during the final orgy, where Fellini has cracked the whip at the whole of Western civilisation, we hear *Patricia. I* tried to say something similar in the context of today's intellectual Bengal in *Subarnarekha. I* have used the same music in the scene at the bar as a Comment,, writes Ghatak.16

Ketan Mehta *(Mirch Masala),* Prakash Jha *(Damul, Mrityudand),* Kalpana Lajmi *(Rudaali),* Govind Nihalani *(Party),* Kumar Shahani *(Tarang)* have made creative use of sound by detailing both is social and aesthetic elements. Shahani has experimented with flat speech patterns, aboslutely without variations in tone, loudness or pitch in his films *Maya Darpan* and*Char Adhyay.* Mani Kaul has dynamised the use of sound in Indian cinema. He has tried to explore it at multiple levels of intelligibility. He plays around the middle-spectrum and changes ones while laying or relaying tracks. He has changed the concept of soundmatching. In Uski Rod, long spells of silence in the narrative and cinematic footage substantiates the loneliness of te wife as she waits for her husband to come home, or, to collect his lunch. Mani Kaul's films are the most significant for the use of nonlinear sound narratives in Indian cinema. In his film *Nazar,* there are no live sounds in the film. But it has long ambiences of sounds that evoke the idea of simultaneity of melody. 17 In his latest film, Mani Kaut is reported to have experimented with new, micro sized, pickup microphones stuck to the body of the actors in his film. These microphones will pick up the body vibrations of the characters as they move, which is apart from the other sound paraphernalia used for speech, music, sound effects and so on.

PART II

The Meaning of Culture

In its most general sense, culture is the whole way of life of a people that is transmitted from one generation to the next. The concept "culture" is often used interchangeably with "society." But society refers to interacting people who *share* a culture, while culture is the *product* of that interaction. Thus, this limited meaning of culture is an abstraction. In everyday speech, culture is often interpreted as refinement or sophistication in the arts. Sociologists and anthropologists commonly define culture as the social product of a human group or society which includes values, language, knowledge and material objects. The people of any group or society share "non material" meanings of what is right and wrong, good and bad, some medium of communication; and knowledge about the environment and about ways of doing things. They also share a body of "material" or physical objects, such as tools, money, clothing, and works of art that reflect nonmaterial cultural meanings. Not only is culture *shared* but it must also be *learned* by each new generation through the process of social interaction. In

India, mainstream cinema is the most immediate and popular process through which social interaction can and does take place.

The Hindi mainstream film and culture:

Perhaps, the most important social function of the Hindi film is its ability to act as an interface between the traditions of Indian society and the*disturbing* modem or Western intrusions into it. At this plane, the Hindi film is a means of (a) giving cultural meaning to Western structures superimposed on society, (b) demystifying some of the culturally" unacceptable modem structures which are increasingly in vogue in India and (c) ritually neutralizing those elements of the modem world which have to be accepted for reasons of survival.'9 But are Western intrusions into the Hindi mainstream film. ethos really *disturbing?* One would not believe so because the emphasis is not on the inner struggle between modernity and tradition. Nor is it on any deep ambivalence towards the West. The function of the Hindi film, according to Shyam. Benegal, a noted Indian film maker, is to externalize an inner psychological conflict and handle the inner passion generated by social and political processes as problems created by events and persons outside. These events and persons are both ideal types and representatives of different aspects of a fragmented self These fragments are separately controlled and the Hindi mainstream seeks to sustain this control by sharpening the focuses of these differences the hero and the anti-hero, the heroine and the antiheroine, the largehearted fatherinlaw and the middleaged don. The Hindi mainstream does this because integration of these separate fragments into a unified whole would highlight the gray elements of characterization which it does not wish to adhere to.

The Indianness of Mainstream Cinema :

But the question is not about *what* culture mainstream Indian films produce. We know the culture it produces is defined and redefined by the time, the place and the socio political context in which it functions. Not to leave out the basic question of economic viability without which the industry's very existence stands to be threatened. The question is about its own cultural *identity.* Does Indian mainstream cinema have a cultural identity that is predominantly and obviously *Indian?* Or, has it become rather hybrid with influences of Hollywood pervading the screen with sexual innuendoes and graphic violence? Is the *Indianness* of Indian cinema under threat of succumbing to the commercially motivated pressures of external values and norms? Or is it being redefined by the stimulus it receives from the Western, specifically Hollywood brand of cinema? All answers to these questions are undercut by the fact that culture itself is in a constant state of flux because it is being influenced and determined by the changes that are taking place in our social, economic and political domains. Culture is not a rigid, static word that defies It does not exist in a vacuum. Nor is it bound anymore within the framework of geographical parameters which are themselves constantly threatened by modern warfare and communicational globalisation via the electronic media. Culture therefore, is itself "hybrid" in its sense of defiance of all *Western* notions of what constitutes "Indian Culture"

It is also hybrid in the way it resists all *Indian* academic attempts to entrap it within predetermined concepts and preconceived notions of scholastic terminology.

Culture has initially meant, in our context, the monuments of antiquity, the temple sculpture of a glorious past, the texts of ancient scriptures, all "the wonder that was." So when we turn to look at presentday cultural practices, weighed down as we are, by the golden past and therefore, by a certain notion of culture, we react with incomprehension, dismissal, embarassment or shame. Is it, perhaps, the very modernity of our culture that prompts this realisation?20

The Language Divide:

In terms of language, though Hindi was, and still is, the principal *lingua franca* for Indian films, the talking picture drew upon target audiences marked by the linguistic divide. Indian films are today made in 17 different languages. The earliest talkies used Hindusthani which was a strange blend of pure Hindi and pure Urdu. Today, we have Hindi films using regionally accented Hindi in the dialogue such as the Bambaiya Hindi which uses a vulgarised version of Hindi spoken in Mumbai. Or, the Telugustressed Hindi spoken by characters set against a Telugu backdrop. Such as in Shyam Benegal's film *Ankur.* There are dialectical versions of Hindi too, as spoken by illiterate tribals, such as in Govind Nihalani's *Aakrosh.* The tone, the pitch, timbre, rhythm and even singsong notes of dialogue delivery vary from region to region, and from different pockets within the same region. Besides, Indian films have the unique quality of different characters speaking different varieties of Hindi according to their social status, their caste, communal identity, education, profession, financial status, etc. Thus, within the same film, you have the educated hero speaking very good Hindi peppered with impeccable English when needs be. The heroine, if she is semiliterate and comes from a rural setting, speaks in some dialectical, hybridised form of Hindi to suit the costume she is wearing, which reflects the region she seems to come from. The villain's goons, speak in a special vulgarised, Bambaiya (from Bombay) Hindi concocted specifically to typify such screen characters in Hindi cinema. If there is an Indian Christian character, specially a female, she speaks her lines in a typical Goan-accented Hindi stressing the long vowels with her grammar all wrong. This, even if she is not really from Goa today, writes :

In Prakash Jha's *Damul* (Death by Hanging) the dialogue is a rustic Bihari dialect. It is easy to understand and is also symbolic often simplicity of the village folk. At the same time, the powerful people in the village intersperse their lines with heavily accented English words like *kundidate, dangerous problem* and uppojishun. This shows the political awareness of vested interests. These days, a lot of English crops into the dialogue and songs of Hindi mainstream films, since in the larger metros, English is as popular and as common as Hindi among the upperclass, urban and educated class. English phrases like "I Love You" and sentences like "CAT *CAT, Cat Maane Billi,* RAT Rat, *Rat Maane Chooha" (CAT* means 'cat' and RAT means 'rat') often form the lyrics of film songs.

Chidananda Dasgupta, the seniormost and most scholastic film critic in the country

"The 'Hindi' film is a misnomer. "The language in most of the productions grouped under this rubric is Hindustani, with a bias towards Urdu. The official 'national' language, with its predilection for shuddh *(pure) Hindi, is far removed from what passes muster with the populace. The businessman out to make money has succeeded in determining the practical possibilities of an allIndia language of a culturally underdeveloped (low literacy, violence against women and low castes and religious orthodoxy) area, naturally susceptible to totalist promptings, on relatively superior cultures. The film industry's interest lies in the widest possible accetpability for the eclectic, open language its products use in selling themselves to all corners of the country. Thus, the Hindi film is accepted in the northeastern states where English enjoys predominance, in the south where local languages hold sway, in the east, in Orissa which has a rich and old history, and in Bengal, where Bengali literature has reached very high levels of contemporary consciousness. ,21*

The Musical Metaphor:

Music in Indian cinema is unique in its cultural implications because it spells out the Indianness of cinema even when the songs or the background score are influenced, inspired and now, even plagiarised from Western, African and Arabic hits. Music in Indian mainstream cinema defines a new synthesis of traditional and international genres of music. Each level involves such a synthesis that any one particular level cannot simply be reduced to another. A cinema song cannot be reduced to its classical or folk roots. The fact that a particular film song is based on a classical *raaga* or on a folk tune does not deny it its distinct genreidentity. As film music grew, it became clear that good composers of film music would of neccessity, have to be trained within the musical ambience of Hindi cinema itself. Though earlier grounding in classical and folk forms offer sound support to music directors, a truly loyal and committed music composer for mainstream films must seek inspiration from the kinetic visuals of cinema. Today's music director often does just this.

Classical and folk Indian music are intimately tied to our feudal, historical past. The essential function of folk music is to glue individuals into a group to perform ritualised functions. Folk music tends to be collectivist, tied as it is, to rural life where functions are collective and songs are sung mainly in groups. Classical music on the other hand, invokes and celebrates the grandeur of power and aristocracy. Its main aim is to distance the mind from worldly cares and material pleasures in favour of abandoning oneself to the love of spiritualism and of dedication. It is therefore, estranged from the world of reality and consequently, from the masses. Indian film music is said to be the ideal adaptive response of Indian culture to the technologyinspired, jetlike pace of the 20th Century. Unwittingly, Hindi film songs have created and underscored democratic values of equality and freedom, of patriotism and secularity, of love and brotherhood and solidarity.

Songs and dances in popular Indian cinema are used as natural expressions of everyday emotions and situations. While seeking to intensify the element of fantasy through music and spectacle, popular cinema also reinforces the impression that songs and dances are the natural and logical expression of emotion in a given situation within the filmic; narrative. This coincides, to a large extent, to the Indian social reality where music forms an integral part of life itself, whether it be in celebration of a happy event like a birth in the family, or a wedding, or, when the occasion is one of grief such as a death within the home. Music contributes a vital ingredient in the cultural reconstruct of emotion. Popular cinema however, has learnt to adapt it to suit to the changing demands of an increasingly global audience through exaggeration, plagiarisation, adaptation of Western fads like rap, and has placed it against spectacle.

No modem musical form from any part of the globe, including jazz, can boast of such diversity, richness, subtlety and reach as the Hindi film song can. 22 The Hindi film song has cut through all language barriers in India to engage in lively communication with a nation where more than 20 languages are spoken. Whether the film is a family melodrama, a historical adventure, a mythological tale, a comedy, a love story or a thriller, songs arc bound to be part of each finished film. Exceptions to the golden rule were sometimes made with drastic results at the box office. To mention a couple, B.R.Chopra's courtroom drama *Kanoon* and his murder mystery *Ittefaq* were both without songs in them. *Kanoon* did break even but that was mainly because of its star value and imaginative cinematography than because it was songless. *Ittefaq* flopped and the same goes for K.A.Abbas' film*Munna*. But all these films had rich background scores to express theme, mood and ambience. Prakash Jha's offmainstream film *Damul* *is* also songless. The background score is amply infused with atmosphere and mood. For atmosphere, you hear the humming of crickets in the night. For mood, there are sounds of pathetic of the *basti* women, which sounds like moaning the dead. The sound of drums heightens the tension of a tense scene. Since the director claims that the entire film was shot in natural light, in the semidarkness of the evening and night shots, the sounds acquire loudness and clarity, underscoring the 'reality' of the tragic circumstances of the oppressed people.

PART III

The Culturespecific Character of Sound in Indian Cinema

Sounds in Indian Cinema:

Sound in Indian cinema has a specific *rhythm* which is unique unto itself The 'sound design' of an entire film is composed of speech, music, songs, noise and silence. The average Indian film. has a stereotypical 'sound design' which is reflective of the Indian ethos and the Indian culture. Irrespective of its generic classification, this sound has the following common characteristics:

- **background score** theme music, musical motif signifying the entry of a specific character, mood music, etc.

- **songs -** theme song repeated over the narrative space of the film, songs lip synched by the characters in the film in solo or in ducts, chorus songs, songs sung to dance numbers, mood songs on the soundtrack and so on. Sometimes, the same song is repeated in varying tempos to signify the changing mood of the character and the changed situation in the storyscript. Most importantly, there are purely soundcentric, and soundbased songs in Indian films where the lyrics of a song are peppered with actual *sounds* such as

(a) the sound of quickened heart beats (dhak dhak karne laga from *Beta)*

(b) the sound of thundering rain (lapaka jhapaka tu aare bbadarava from *Boot Polish),*

(c) the sound of the spinning wheel (chappa chappa charkha chale from *Maachis),*

(d) the sound of dancing bells **Ghanak jhanak payal baaje from***Jhanak Jhanak Payal Baaje* and **chhamma chhamma, baaje re mori paayaiiya from** *China Gate*

(e) the sound (?) of night Ghoom jhoom dhalti raat in *K6hraa),*

(f) the sound(?) of tears (naina barase, rimjhim rimjhim in *Woh Kaun*ThO),(g) the sound of lapping waves on the shores (chhai chhapa chhai, chhapapa chhai in Hu Tu Tu), (

h) song to match the beat and rhythm of a running train in a hilly terrain (chal chhaiyyan chhaiyan in *Dil Se* ...),

(i) the sound of the singing nightingale (kuhu kuhu bole koyeliyaan in*Rani Roopmati)* and so on, offering a rich texture and a neverending panorama of sounds within songs, making for an unique blend of sound, music and song. Usually combined with colourful visuals and harmoniously choreographed dances, these songs add both to the market value of the film at the box office and to the final audiovisual effect the film leaves behind.

- **dialogue** if this is a voiceover, or an interior monologue, it is usually sombre, soft spoken, articulate, with clear enunciation. If this is a dialogue, it is generally longwinded and wordy, loud and highpitched, alternating between the ornamental and the crude, with shades in between. The accents of different kinds of Hindi create varied sound effects. Because of the multiple-language culture, no cinema in the world offers the variety in dialogue, speech, monologue, etc, that Indian cinema offers. Voiceovers by female characters are a rarity in Indian films. Two out of a handful of specific exceptions however, are Satyajit Ray's *Ghare Baire* (Me Home and the World) and Rituparno Ghosh's *Dahan.* One brilliant example of ways of speech, enunciation and designing of silence, along with special sound effects to generate and ambience of fear, is the mainstream offering *Sholay* (Flames) directed by Ramesh Sippy. Sippy took special pains to draw out different speech patterns to suit the different characters in this film each character's personality being defined by his/her distinct manner of dialoguedelivery, tone, voice and pitch. The director offered sound counterpoints through the two major female characters, one extremely talkative and the other totally silent, offering another sound design which invests the film with an unusual richness. The silent girl is shown to have been very talkative through flashbacks, as a young and filmloving maiden. The present time-frame projects her as having withdrawn into a self-imposed shell of silence, postwidowhood. The sound of speech of dialogue in Indian cinema, is a highly subjective exercise.

- noise In his essay, *Notes for an Aesthetic of Cinema Sound,* Kumar Shahani says that incidental and atmospheric sounds in cinema lie between organised sound (music) drifting into entropy and contextual sounds (speech), while the rest is silence. Sound defined thus, needs to be classified differently.

Cinema has always been a reflection of the ethos and ideology of any society at a given point of time. The mediums to accentuate this reflection varied from costumes to music to items of luxury; but the most crucial medium became the characters. The mind-set, thinking, apprehensions or the prejudices of the characters were the same as those of the general public.

The same theory applied to the portrayal of female characters as well. To start with, women who chose the unconventional profession of acting were looked down upon as prostitutes or women who were "easily available." Although, later movies like *Mother India* were made in which <u>Nargis Dutt</u> played a more challenging and substantial role, the basis of the portrayal remained the same.

The ideal woman was depicted to be submissive and shy, dependent and fragile, usually clad in a sari, whereas the famous vamps of Bollywood donned bold outfits. Women who dressed in a style more influenced by the West were usually considered to be morally degraded. If we look at the 1970s or '80s, the favourite vamps of that era like <u>Bindu</u>, <u>Helen</u> or <u>Aruna Irani</u> were some of the first women to smoke, drink or engage in pre-marital sex onscreen, unlike other actresses. Such activities were a sign that the women characters had questionable morals, though when a male actor did the same onscreen he was seen as being macho. The actresses on the other hand would not even dare to do so as they were expected to be docile, shy and dependent womenbecause these were the virtues of a "well-cultured" Indian woman. This is one of the reasons why many eyebrows were raised when <u>Sharmila Tagore</u> became the first woman to wear a bikini in the movie *An Evening in Paris*in 1967, and when *Zeenat Aman* kissed onscreen in the movie *Heera Panna*. In the '80s, women started to be taken a little more seriously which was reflected in a few women-centric movies like *Umrao Jaan* and *Paakizah*.

In the '90s their roles were beginning to change drastically—they became more substantial. Being an actress became much more than just playing eye candy and dancing around trees. One of the best examples of this was actress Seema Biswas's role in the movie Bandit Queen in 1994. She portrayed the character of a woman who was far more than the docile and fragile figures of the 80s. She was strong, courageous and had the ability to take on twenty men alone. All this was happening simultaneously with the changing roles of women in the Indian society. Women were getting liberated and independent. They were better educated and had innumerable employment opportunities and this was reflected in Indian cinema.

But it was the films released in the first decade of the 21st century that redefined the Indian woman in the world of cinema. From movies like *Astitva*, *Lajja* , *Chandani Bar* and *Page 3* in the early years to *Dor*, *Turning 30*, *Fashion* and <u>No One Killed Jessica</u> in the latter half of the Noughties, their characters were as strong as that of the male protagonists, but more profound. She could be anything from a shrewd politician to a bold journalist to a prostitute or a super-successful entrepreneur. The role of the Indian female was revolutionised in cinema— just like in real life. She became this fierce, successful, dominating, independent and ultramodern woman of today.

Although, there is no particular way of portraying the Indian woman onscreen in Indian cinema, it is very evident that their roles run parallel to the roles women get to play in the society at particular points in time. Therefore, if we compare andanalyse the journey of women in Indian cinema today, there is no doubt in the fact that the" Indian woman" has come a long way not only in reel life, but also in real life.

In the journey of 100 years, Indian cinema has come a long way and so the women character. Showing many shades, the portrayal of women not only touched the lives of the audiences but also showcased the strength, beauty and complexity that define a woman. Jasleen Kaur takes a walk down the memory lane with some of the characters.

Since its inception 100 years ago, commercial cinema has always been one of the biggest indigenous industries in India and remains so in the post-globalisation era, when the Indian economy has entered a new phase of global participation, liberalisation and expansion. Issues of community, gender, society, social and economic justice, secular nationhood and ethnic identity are nowhere more explored in the Indian cultural mainstream than in commercial cinema. It is unmatched and penned out a proud history for itself. From the black and white films to colour movies, even if the Indian cinema has evolved in a big way, today it continuous to retain its basic essence – entertain, entertain and entertain. Even as internet downloads and television continue to cannibalize the theatrical revenues of Indian films, the lure of the 35 mm is something else altogether. Indian cinema has come a long way and concurrently, has witnessed a sea-change in the presentation of the women character. From the very first film, Raja Harishchandra – which had no female actors – to the modern day, it has not been an easy ride. And one reason for this can be the 'beauty' which has evolved over time in Indian cinema. Actresses like Madhuabala, Wahida Rehman and Vaijayantimala were considered the queens of the Indian cinema during their reign. Then came the southern beauties who ruled the Bollywood like Hema Malini and Rekha. In 1994, the beauty queen Aishwarya Rai, after crowned the beauty pageant, entered the film fraternity and won millions of Indians fell in love with her.

Straight-jacketed limits

For so long, Indian cinema was undoubtedly male dominated. Themes were used to be explored from the male audience's point of view and actress was considered secondary to the actor. Her role was used to chart out in the context of any male character that was central to the story line– be it hero, villain,father, boss or an elderly male figure. She was devoid of any independent existence. This kind of straightjacketing limits the women's role to provide glamour, relief, respite and entertainment. And these patriarchal values were institutionalized in films like Dahej (1950), Gauri (1968), Devi (1970), Biwi ho to Aisi (1988), Pati Parmeshwar (1988) depicted women as passive, submissive wives as perfect figures and martyrs for their own families.

Larger than life roles

Earlier, they used to portray larger than life characters. They rather than being depicted as normal human beings were elevated to a higher position of being ideal who can commit no wrong. Their grievances, desires, ambitions, feelings, perspectives were completely missing from the scene. They were shown as not belonging to this real and worldly life. Amitabh and Jaya Bachchan starrer Abhimaan (1973) began with premise of the wife (Jaya) being more talented than the husband (Amitabh). This in itself is a defiance of the stereotype. However, the film crumbled from then on when the wife gave up her thriving musical career for satisfying the husband's ego culminating to a conventional closure that demands adherence to traditional values of marriage and motherhood.

In decorative capacity

The other face which was criticised as the character of women in the silver screen is the decorative capacity. What we got to see was feminine shadows in the background – wives, mothers, sisters, sweethearts and vamps playing second-fiddle to the male protagonists. Film scholar and author Shoma Chatterji, said, "Women in Hindi cinema have been decorative objects with rarely any sense of agency being imparted to them. Each phase of Hindi cinema had its own representation of women, but they were confined largely to the traditional, patriarchal framework of the Indian society. The ordinary woman has hardly been visible in Hindi cinema."

It has commonly seen in the action-packed movies of Akshay Kumar, Sunny Deol and Sunil Shetty; the actress was abruptly placed in the romantic track as a distraction for the viewer from monotonous bouts of violence. So, the moot question is how real were the women characters in the movies? This is something to debate about because values, ideals, principles; morals have dominated the framework in which these films are placed.

Whenever a woman is shown, she is shown satisfying men's desires and is portrayed as raw material for producing and rearing children. The women characters, even after getting Master's Degree in Science, succumb to observance of the rituals like 'Karava Chauth', the fasting for longer life of husband. The girls, who are shown in the barest possible outfits until they are married, are denied to have 'say' while choosing their life partners. The parents, the custodian of traditions, do that job for them. After getting married these women are mindlessly loaded with the weight of bangles, ornaments, and conventional clothes. Such a turnaround, while artistically displayed on screen, thins the morale of the girls who want to be the captains of their own boats.

Real woman has emerged

Gone are the days when the realself of Indian women hardly matches with the script. Today, it will rarely anyone say that Indian cinema has been essentially male-centric, leaving little space for the female counterparts to evolve and grow as versatile performers. As now we have been seeing increasing numbers of movies creating bold and beautiful of Bollywood, in the past also, we've had actresses portraying strong characters who fight the shackles of their social milieu and the very first film is Mother India released in 1957. Considered as one of the finest classics of Indian cinema, the movie looks at the struggle of a rural woman in India, who fights all odds to raise her two sons. The portrayal of the late actress Nargis Dutt is of a loving and brave mother, who struggles to raise her family alone and in the end, saying true to her cause, she kills her evil son to save a woman's honour.

Women in Indian cinema are born with certain assumptions ranging from cult movies to celluloid blockbusters like Sholay to more recent Fashion that employ themselves as in severe gender issues. They are portrayed either as damsels in distress or demented feminists or simple bellyshaking glam dolls whose sole ambition is to attract the attention of the male gender. In many Indian films it is a common trend to insert 'item numbers' which bear no rational connection to the film in anyways but with an assumption that the film is easily associated. Sometimes the one song ends up making a mark for the film, such as 'Munni' from

Dabangg, 'Chikni Chameli' of Agneepath or 'Fevicol' of Dabangg 2.

In order to present the modernity among women, Indian filmmakers have arachuted on an idea that the display of dancing girls in 'minimum' clothes isreal expression of freedom. On a lighter note, our elder generation, earlier exposed to the "sensuous" Helen, is now face-to-face with the more "fatal" Bipasha Basu. Many are saying that the change is 'delicious for their 'filmy' palate!

Actress Sonam Kapoor told to an American Publication, "Unfortunately, things have actually gone downhill since the golden era of the sixties which had great films with such beautiful portrayals of women (such as Bandhini and Sujata). Back then, male actors were not afraid to put actresses in the forefront with these characters. But during the eighties, it went downhill as women were usually objectified and shown as props in the film. But the industry became male-dominated through the nineties and even now, to an extent, with the item song culture. There are exceptions today as well with actress Vidya Balan's roles in Kahaani and No One Killed Jessica. And she did a great job in The Dirty Picture, which showed how women were portrayed in eighties cinema. But today, the really big films — those which cross the coveted rupees one billion mark at the box office — objectify women."

In the present day, the typical Indian woman, item number and individualism share an almost symbiotic relationship. These three ingredients have become the major part of Indian cinema. Gone are the days when stories were written about the shy village girls or the ethical beauty, these are the times for rebellious lovers and sexy and confident business women who rule the roost. The stereotypical portrayal of women, which ruled Indian films till a very recent time, has been witnessing a remarkable change – be it the blood thirsty Priyanka from 7 Khoon Maaf, or no nonsense journalist Rani in No One Killed Jessica or Parineeti Chopra as the rebellious lover from Ishaqzaade, each of their characters stood apart from the conventional women and none of them had qualms about it.

For that matter Fashion, although the movie depicts the inside of the fashion industry it primly revolves around the life of Meghan Mathur who is dejected by the society, yet she comes back with new élan and enthusiasm. Besides Fashion, the female characters in Madhur Bhandarkar's films are usually shown as bold and empowered women who lead life on their own terms, take their own decisions, are 'rebels' who don't conform to social norms and excel in their respective professions like Chandni Bar (2001), Page 3 (2005), and the latest one Kareena Kapoor starrer Heroine.

Actresses like Vidya Balan (Paa, Dirty Picture, Kahani, Ishqiya) and Konkona Sen Sharma (Page 3, Wake Up Sid, Life in a Metro, Mr. and Mrs. Iyer) have led this change of direction, who have appeared in strong and independent roles which for the time being shifted the camera's focus from the women's body to her identity as an individual.

What recently has happened is in the light of recent incident of gangrape that shook the entire nation, Bollywood as a part of popular culture, has come under the scanner for commodification of women. In a freewheeling chat at the set of CNN IBN, the cast (Arjun Rampal and Chitrangada Singh) and director (Sudhir Mishra) of movie Inkaar which deals with a very sensitive issue of sexual harassment at work places, were present to talk about the social responsibility of cinema and the portrayal of women in Bollywood. The director said that it's not necessary that what Bollywood preaches, the nation follows. In fact, at times, the film industry reflects what is happening in society for real. While, micro blogging sites like Twitter are still abuzz with how item songs in films often objectify women, she pointed out that dance and songs are very important part of Indian cinema and are mostly added only for entertainment value. If a particular song-dance sequence shows a woman being stalked and wooed by a bunch of men in a playful and romantic manner and she is enjoying the attention that she is getting then it in no way sends out a wrong signal.

The portrayal of women in cinema is slowly becoming real, no longer a figment of imagination. The characters have become close to reality, if not the reality itself. We no longer go to the cinemas to find an alternate reality, we no more witness the village belle who is afraid to speak her mind rather a women who can win her way through the crowd, most often we identify ourselves with the characters onscreen and the reflection of reality is nonetheless a perk in transformed filmmaking. The veteran filmmaker Mahesh Bhatt said on the occasion of the International Women's Day, "In India, we can't make sweeping statements claiming that the portrayal of women in Bollywood has progressed or regressed. As a director, I have always made films giving the women center stage. Conservatives and vested groups have often claimed that the women in my recent films have been scantily clad or are overtly sexual. However, they can't deny that the women in my films have been in charge of their own destiny. Now women can live life with dignity, without relying on a man for support. At the same time, it made Shabana a national icon. Another person who embodies the new Indian woman is Vidya Balan."

<u>Greatest Base Persons in Indian cinema</u>

1.   **Dilip Kumar:**

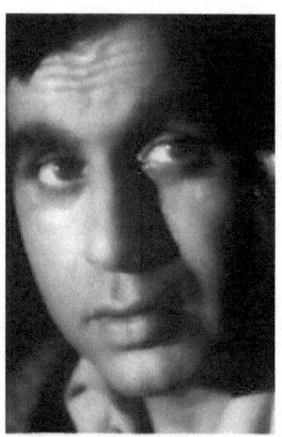

Dilip Kumar is considered to be one of the greatest actors of Indian cinema. Starting his career in 1944, he has starred in some of the biggest commercially successful films in the period 1949-1961. . He was the first actor to receive a Filmfare Best Actor Award and holds the record for most number of Filmfare Awards won for that category. Though he has done films of other genres occasionally like - he balanced out with roles such as the intense Andaz (1949) with the swashbuckling Aan (1952), the dramatic Devdas (1955) with the comical Azaad (1955) and the historical romance Mughal E Azam (1960) with the social Ganga Jamuna (1961), he pre-dominantly specialized in doing love stories or tragic roles from 1944-1961. From late 1960s roles dried up for Kumar as films starring Dev Anand, Rajendra Kumar and Shammi Kapoor were more successful from 1961-1969 and also Dilip's films from 1966 to 1976 were box office flops like Dil Diya Dard Liya, Sunghursh, Aadmi, Dastaan, Gopi, Sagina and Bairaag and after 1976 he left films for a five year break. After Rajesh Khanna became first superstar of Indian Cinema in 1969, most of the author backed lead roles from 1969-1991, went to Rajesh Khanna. In 1981 Dilip returned with a character role at insistence of Manoj Kumar in the blockbuster film Kranti and continued his career playing central character roles in multi-hero films such as Shakti (1982), Karma (1986), Vidhaata, Mazdoor, Mashaal, Duniya, Dharm Adhikari, Kanoon Apna Apna, Izzatdaar, Saudagar (1991), Qila. But his only films to be successful from 1981 at box office were Kranti, Vidhaata, Karma, Dharm Adhikari, Kanoon Apna Apna and Saudagar. He has retired from the Indian Film Industry in 1998.

He was born Muhammad Yusuf Khan in Qissa Khawani Bazaar in Peshawar Pakistan in a Pashtun family of twelve children. His father Ghulam Sarwar was a fruit merchant and owned large orchards in Peshawar and Devlali in Maharashtra near Mumbai. The family relocated to Mumbai in 1930s and in the early 1940s Yusuf Khan moved to Pune and started off with his canteen business and supplying dry fruits.

There he was spotted by a leading actress of those years Devika Rani who was also the wife of the founder of Bombay Talkies Himanshu Rai and helped his entry into the Bollywood film industry. She also gave him the screen name of Dilip Kumar.

His first film Jwar Bhata, was released in 1944 which went unnoticed and his next 2 films Pratima (1945),Naukadubi (1947) were box office flops. In 1947 he shot to prominence with the film Jugnu which was his first major hit and followed it up with successful Shaheed (1948) and thereby became a star.His next release Ghar Ki Izzat(1948) was box office flop. He fell in love with Kamini Kaushal and their on-screen paid was a hit with audience. Kamini Kaushal-Dilip Kumar gave hits like Shaheed(1948), Nadiya Ke Paar (1948),Shabnam (1949), Arzoo (1950). Kamini Kaushal was a bigger star than Dilip Kumar even before they did their first film Shaheed(1948) as a pair, since Kamini had 4 hits to her name already and Dilip had a crush on her ever since her first film Neecha Nagar became a hit in 1946. In 1949, he co-starred with the then struggling actor-director Raj Kapoor, who had a flop in Aag as a director and had 11 flops as an actor before this film, in the romantic melodrama film Andaz, which went to become a huge success and made him a star. Throughout the 1950s he was one of the biggest stars of Bollywood along with Raj Kapoor and Dev Anand. Dev Anand, who had 3 flops from 1946-47, became a star when Ziddi became a hit in 1948 and Raj Kapoor's fortune as an actor changed when Andaz became a hit in 1949.Thus among the trio, first to become a star was Dilip Kumar and then second was Dev Anand and then Raj Kapoor. Dilip became known for playing tragic love story roles in hit films such as Nadiya Ke Paar (1948), Mela (1948), Andaz (1949), Jogan (1950), Babul (1950), Arzoo (1950), Deedar (1951), Tarana (1951), Deedar (1951), Daag (1952), Shikast (1953) which earned him the title of "Tragedy King". . Some of his most famous films in tragic roles were box office flops like Amar (1954), Devdas (1955), Dil Diya Dard Liya (1966) and Aadmi (1968). Madhumati (1958) gave him Filmfare Award for Best Actor.

With Nargis he had 5 hits like Mela (1948),Andaz (1949),Jogan (1950),Babul (1950),Deedar (1951) and 2 flops like Anokha Pyar (1948),Hulchul (1951). In 1951, Kamini Kaushal-Dilip Kumar affair ended. The pair of Madhubala-Dilip Kumar had a hit in Tarana(1951) and 2 flops in Sangdil (1952) and Amar (1954) but the couple fell in love with each-other while working in Amar(1954).Later Madhubala and Dilip Kumar broke up in 1957, while working in Mughal -E-Azam but being professionals did work together to complete the film,which took years to finish and got released in 1960.

From 1952-1961, he had hits like Daag (1952), Aan (1953) and Uran Khatola (1955) with Nimmi, Shikast (1953) with Nalini Jaywant, Foot Path (1953),Azaad (1955), Yahudi (1958) and Kohinoor (1960) with Meena Kumari, Insaniyat (1955) with Bina Rai,Naya Daur (1957),Madhumati (1958) and Ganga Jamuna (1960) with Vyjanthimala, Musafir (1957) with Suchitra Sen. From 1952-1962, his only flops were Sangdil

(1952),Amar (1954),Devdas (1955). So this period of 1949-1961 is considered the peak period of Dilip Kumar's career as a hero.

He was also successful in playing lighthearted roles such as playing a swashbuckling peasant in Aan (1952) and a comic role in Azaad (1955). In 1960 he starred in the historical film Mughal-e-Azam opposite Madhubala, which is as of 2008, the third highest grossing film in Hindi film history inflation adjusted [behind Kismet(1943), Haathi Mere Saathi(1971) and ahead of Sholay(1975), Hum Aapke Hai Kaun(1994)] in which he played the role of the Mughal crown-prince Jehangir the son of Akbar.

In 1961 he produced and starred in the hit Ganga Jamuna in which he and his real Life brother Nasir Khan played the title roles. Despite the film success he did not produce any film after this but gave away the script for its Tamil version Iru Dhruvam starring Sivaji Ganesan. Dilip had a narrow brush with international fame in 1962 when British director David Lean offered him the role of

Sherif Ali in his 1962 film, Lawrence of Arabia. However Kumar declined the part citing its a small role for a big hero like him. The role eventually went to Omar Sharif the Egyptian actor. His next films like the critically acclaimed Leader (1964) and critically panned Dil Diya Dard Liya (1966) which were huge box office flops but he bounced back when he played a dual role of twins separated at birth in the film Ram Aur Shyam (1967) which was one of the biggest box office hits of the year. But again his next releases Aadmi (1968),Sunghursh (1968) flopped and Dilip Kumar's acting career as a hero ended as most of the roles which he would have got went to the first Superstar of Indian Cinema - Rajesh Khanna from 1969-1991.

In the period 1969-1976 the career of most of the actors like Rajendra Kumar, Shammi Kapoor, Dilip Kumar and Raj Kapoor as the hero ended with emergence of Rajesh Khanna. Many of Kumar's films like Sunghursh (1968),Aadmi (1968),Dastaan (1972),Gopi (1973),Sagina (1974),

Bairaag(1976) failed at the box office during this period and after the release of his 1976 film Bairaag in which he played triple roles, he took retirement as the hero. But Manoj Kumar ensured that Dilip Kumar made a comeback and put an end to a five year break from acting but offering a role in Kranti in 1981. Initially Dilip Kumar was hesitant to do the role, but Maoj Kumar convinced him to make a comeback.

He made a comeback in 1981 with the multi-starer Kranti which was the biggest hit of the year. He went onto play character roles as an elderly family patriarch or a police officer in films like Shakti (1982), Karma (1986), Vidhaata, Mazdoor, Mashaal, Duniya, Dharm Adhikari, Kanoon Apna Apna, Izzatdaar, Saudagar (1991), Qila. But his only films to be successful from 1981 at box office were Kranti, Vidhaata, Karma, Dharm Adhikari, Kanoon Apna Apna and Saudagar. In his last major successful film, Saudagar (1991) he appeared alongside another legendary actor Raaj Kumar after three decades since they last appeared together in Paigham (1959). In

1992 he won the Filmfare Lifetime Achievement Award.

In 1996 he was supposed to make his directorial debut with a film titled Kalinga, with him and Rajesh Khanna in the lead, but the film was shelved. In 1998 he made his last film appearance to date in the box office flop Qila where in a rare form he played a villainous role. He has since retired from the film industry due to his indifferent health.

Dilip Kumar's younger brother Nasir Khan was also an actor and appeared opposite Dilip in Ganga Jamuna (1961) and Bairaag (1976) as well as acted as hero in 22 films from 1948-1961, but 17 were flops. Thus Nasir's career was not as successful and he died in 1974. Nasir Khan's son Ayub Khan is also an actor in the industry. Nasir Khan's wife was 1950s actress Begum Para who made a comeback to films after 50 years in the film Saawariya in 2007 in supporting role.

Dilip Kumar married actress and "beauty queen" Saira Banu in 1966 when he was aged 44 and she was 22. At the time, gossip columnists predicted doom for the high-profile couple, but the union has been one of the longest lasting marriages in Bollywood.

2. **Satyajit Ray:**

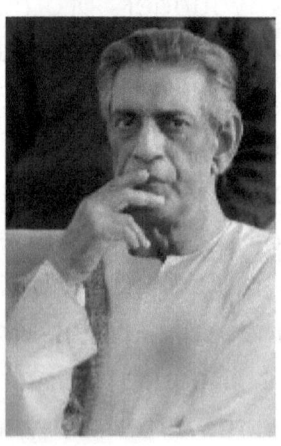

Satyajit Ray was an Indian filmmaker, regarded as one of the greatest auteurs of world cinema. Ray was born in the city of Calcutta into a Bengali family prominent in the world of arts and literature. Starting his career as a commercial artist, Ray was drawn into independent filmmaking after meeting French filmmaker Jean Renoir and viewingVittorio De Sica's Italian neorealist 1948 film *Bicycle Thieves* during a visit to London.

Ray directed 36 films, including feature films, documentaries and shorts. He was also a fiction writer, publisher, illustrator, calligrapher, music composer, graphic designer and film critic. He authored several short stories and novels, primarily aimed at children and adolescents. Feluda, the sleuth, and Professor Shonku, the scientist in his science fiction stories, are popular fictional characters created by him.He was awarded honorary doctorate by the Oxford University and he was the second after Charlie Chaplin.

Ray's first film, *Pather Panchali* (1955), won eleven international prizes, including *Best Human Documentary* at the Cannes Film Festival. This film, *Aparajito* (1956), and *Apur Sansar* (1959) form *The Apu Trilogy*. Ray did the scripting, casting, scoring, and editing, and designed his own credit titles and publicity material. Ray received many major awards in his career, including 32 IndianNational Film Awards, a number of awards at international film festivals and award ceremonies, and an honorary Academy Award in 1992. The Government of India honoured him with the Bharat Ratna in 1992.

3.   **Guru Dutt:**

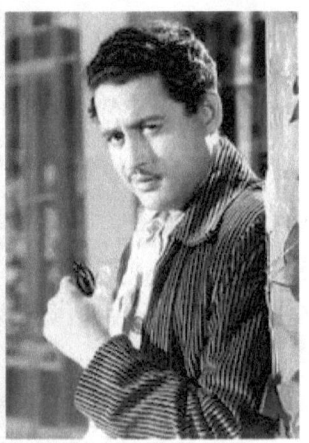

Considered to be a man ahead of his time, Guru Dutt was one of the greatest icons of commercial Indian cinema. Although he made less than 50 films during his lifetime, they are believed to be the best to come from Bollywood's Golden Age, known both for their ability to reach out to the common man and for their artistic and lyrical content, and they went on to become trendsetters that have influenced Bollywood ever since. But for all his genius, there was a shroud of tragedy that overshadowed his career and life.

Dutt was born in Mysore on 9 July 1925, the eldest son of a headmaster and a housewife who was a part-time writer. He did not have a good childhood: he had to deal with a strained relationship between his parents, hostility from his maternal relatives, and the death of a close relative. He received his early education in Calcuta, and in 1941, he joined the Uday Shankar India Culture Center, where he received basic training in the performing arts under dance maestro Uday Shankar. Afterward, in 1944, he had a short stint as a telephone operator.

Dutt entered the Indian film industry in 1944, working as a choreographer in Prabhat Studios. There, he became friends with Dev Anand (whom he met when they worked on the film Hum Ek Hain (1946)) and Rehman. These early friendships helped ease his way into Bollywood. After Prabhat went under in 1947, Dutt moved to Mumbai, where he worked with the leading directors of the time: Amiya

Chakrabarty in Girls' School(1949) and Gyan Mukherjee in Sangram (1946).

He got his big break when Dev Anand invited him to direct a film in his newly formed company Navketan Films. Dutt made his directorial debut with Baazi (1951), which starred Dev Anand. The film was an urban crime thriller that paid homage to classic film noir. However, it also carried its own elements that ensured it was not a remake of a Hollywood film: notably, songs were used to further the story's narrative, and close-up shots were used frequently. The film was a success and became a trendsetter for future crime films. On the personal front, Dutt met his wife, playback singer Geeta Dutt (née Roy), during the song-recording sessions of <u>Baazi</u> (1951), and they married 26th May 1953.

Dutt's next releases were <u>Jaal</u> (1952) and <u>Baaz</u> (1953). Dutt made his acting debut in the latter film, which he also directed. But while they were average successes, he finally tasted success with <u>Aar-Paar</u> (1954), another crime thriller, but with a far more polished story and look. Then came <u>Mr. & Mrs. '55</u> (1955), a frothy romantic comedy focusing on women's' rights; and <u>C.I.D.</u> (1956), yet another crime thriller in which<u>Waheeda Rehman</u> made her debut.

His next films, <u>Pyaasa</u> (1957) and <u>Kaagaz Ke Phool</u> (1959), are regarded as his best work. <u>Pyaasa</u> (1957) was his masterpiece, about a poet trying to achieve success in a hypocritical, uncaring world. It was a box-office hit and is ranked as his greatest film ever. In contrast, <u>Kaagaz Ke Phool</u> (1959) was a miserable flop at the box office: the semi-autobiographical story of a tragic love affair set against the backdrop of the film industry was deemed too morbid for the audience to swallow and went right over audience's heads. Although in later years the film received critical acclaim for its cinematography and has gained a cult following, Dutt, who had put his soul into the film, was devastated over its failure and never directed another film.

Although he had sworn off directing, Dutt continued to

produce and act in films, notably the period dramas <u>Full Moon</u> (1961) and <u>Sahib Bibi Aur Ghulam</u> (1962). The latter film, interestingly, is controversial because it is debated whether Dutt had ghost-directed the film. Unfortunately, Dutt's personal life had become a shambles: he had gotten involved with his protégé <u>Waheeda Rehman</u> and his wife Geeta Dutt had separated from him as a result. Rehman too had distanced herself from him. Also, Dutt, an ambitious person, felt he had achieved too much too soon professionally--there was nothing better to be achieved, and this caused a vacuum in his life. Unable to cope with all the trauma and emptiness, he took to heavy drinking.

On 10 October 1964, Dutt was found dead in his bed. The cause of death was deemed a combination of alcohol and sleeping pills, although a debate still lingers over whether his death was by accident or a successful suicide attempt. Geeta Dutt suffered a nervous breakdown as a result of his death and also took to alcohol, eventually drinking herself to death, dying in 1972 as a result of cirrhosis of the liver.

His death was an irreplaceable loss to Indian cinema. And it was a tragic twist of fate that his films, most of which were discounted in his lifetime, would be regarded as cult classics after his death. Guru Dutt would always be known, even if posthumously, as the Guru of Bollywood's Golden

Age and one of the world's most important international auteurs....

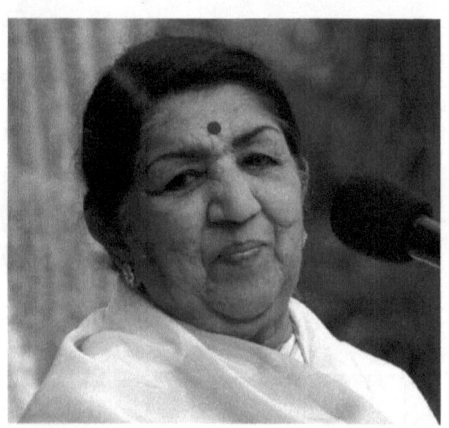

4.   **Lata Mangeskar**

Lata Mangeshkar was born in Indore on September 8, 1929, and became, quite simply, the most popular playback singer in Bollywood's history. She has sung for over 50 years for actresses from <u>Nargis</u> to <u>Preity</u>

Zinta, as well as having recorded albums of all kinds (ghazals, pop, etc). Until the 1991 edition, when her entry disappeared, the Guinness Book of World Records listed her as the most-recorded artist in the world with not less than 30,000 solo, duet,and chorus-backed songs recorded in 20 Indian languages between 1948 and 1987. Today that number might have reached 40,000!

She was born the daughter of Dinanath Mangeshkar, the owner of a theater company and a reputed classical singer in his own right. He started giving Lata singing lessons from the age of five, and she also studied with renowned singers Aman Ali Khan Sahib and Amanat Khan. Even at a young age she displayed a

God-given musical gift and could master vocal exercises the first time.

Ironically, for someone of her stature, she made her entry into Bollywood at the wrong time - around the 1940s, when bass singers with heavily nasal voices, such as <u>Noor Jehan</u> and <u>Shamshad Begum</u> were in style. She was rejected from many projects because it was believed that her voice was too high-pitched and thin. The circumstances of her entry into the industry were no less inauspicious - her father died in 1942, the responsibility of earning income to support her family fell upon her, and between 1942 and 1948 she acted in as many as eight films in Hindi and Marathi to take care of economic hardships. She made her debut as a playback singer in the Marathi film Kiti Hasaal (1942) but, ironically, the song was edited out!

However, in 1948, she got her big break with Ghulam Haider in the film Majboor(1948), and 1949 saw the release of four of her films: Mahal (1949), Dulari (1 949),Barsaat (1949),
and Andaz (1949); all four of them became runaway hits, with their songs reaching to heights of what was until then unseen popularity. Her unusually high-pitched singing rendered the trend of heavily nasal voices of the day totally obsolete and, within a year, she had changed the face of playback singing forever. The only two lower-pitched singers to survive her treble onslaught to a certain extent were Geeta

<u>Dutt</u> and <u>Shamshad   Begum</u>.

Her singing style was initially reminiscent of <u>Noor Jehan</u>, but she soon overcame that and evolved her own distinctive style. Her sister, <u>Asha Bhosle</u>, too, came up in the late 1950s and the two of them were the queens of Indian playback singing right through to the 1990s. Her voice had a special versatile quality, which meant that finally music composers could stretch their creative experiments to the fullest. Although all her songs were immediate hits under any composer, it was the composers <u>C. Ramchandra</u>and <u>Madan Mohan</u> who made her sound her sweetest and challenged her voice like no other music director.

The 1960s and 1970s saw her go from strength to strength, even as there were accusations that she was monopolizing the playback-singing industry. However, in the 1980s, she cut down her workload to concentrate on her shows abroad. Today, Lata sings infrequently despite a sudden resurgence in her popularity, but even today some of Hindi Cinema's biggest hits, including <u>Dilwale Dulhania Le Jayenge</u> (1995), <u>Dil To Pagal Hai</u> (1997), and <u>Veer-Zaara</u> (2004) feature her legendary voice.

No matter which female playback singer breaks through in any generation, she cannot replace the timeless voice of Lata Mangeshkar. She is an icon beyond icons...

5. **Dr. Rajkumar**

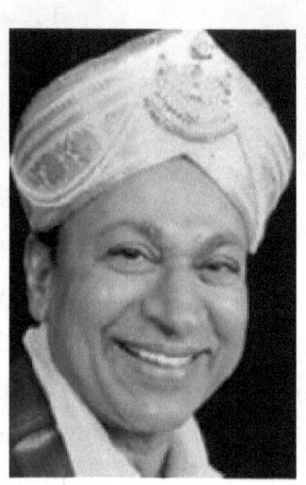

Dr. Rajkumar was born in 1929 in Gajanur and brought up in a poor family. He only studied up to 3rd standard before he dropped out of school. He wanted to follow in the footsteps of his father, a traveling actor who performed in various villages. He joined the Gubbi Veeranna drama company to play drama. There he met people like Narasimhraju, Balakrishna and G.V. Iyer, who co-starred with him in his first film, Bedara Kannappa (1954).

His three sons-- Shivarajkumar, Raghavendra Rajkumar and Puneet Rajkumar--are all Kannada film actors. His other films have included Havina Hede (1981), Dashavtara (1960), Yarivanu? (1984), Kamana Billu (1983) and he had the lead role in Odahuttidavaru (1969). His last film was Shabdavedi (2000). After this movie he declared that he was about to act in another film, "Bhakta Ambareesha", but he suffered a mild heart attack, and decided to retire from acting altogether.

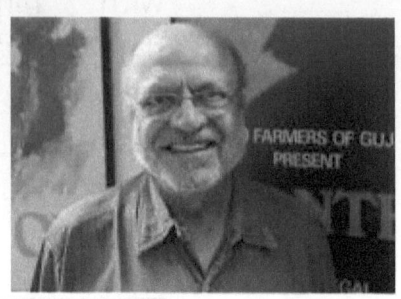

6.   Shyam Benegal

Shyam Benegal was born on December 14, 1934 in Alwal, Hyderabad, British India. He is a director and writer, known for <u>Zubeidaa</u> (2001), <u>Welcome to   Sajjanpur</u> (2008) and<u>Junoon</u> (1979).

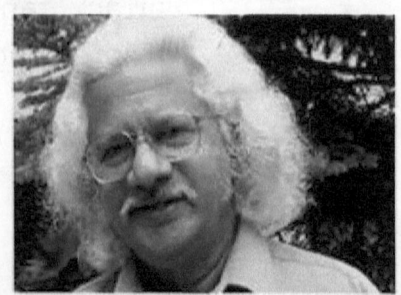

7.   **Adoor Gopalakrishnan**

Adoor Gopalakrishnan is India's most acclaimed contemporary filmmaker. Born in 1941 in Kerala, a state in south India, he belongs to a family with strong links to the performing arts, especially Kathakali, a highly-stylised form of dance drama. From the age of eight Adoor began acting for the stage, later producing and directing over twenty plays, several written by him. He is the author of two books on the theatre as well as a book on the cinema, "The World of Cinema", for which he won a national award in 1983. In 1962 Adoor enrolled in the Film and Television Institute in Pune and graduated in 1965 with a diploma in Scriptwriting and Direction. The same year he founded the Chitralekha Film Society of Trivandrum as well as the Chitralekha Film Cooperative. Both played a key role in the development of film culture in Kerala. In 1972 Adoor made Swayamvaram/One's Own Choice, his first full-length feature film. It launched the New Cinema in Kerala and became one of the major films of the Indian New Wave. He has since made seven more films (along with over 25 shorts and documentaries), all of which have won major national and international awards: Kodiyettam/Ascent (1977); Elippathayam/Rat Trap (1981); Mukhamukham/Face to Face (1984); Anantaram/Monologue (1987); Mathilukal/The Walls

(1990); Vidheyan/The Servile (1993), and Kathapurushan/Man of the Story (1995). Elippathayam received the prestigious British Film Institute Award in 1982; Mukhamukham won the FIPRESCI prize in 1985; Kathapurushan was honoured in India in 1995 with the National Award for Best Film. Retrospectives of Adoor's films have been held in Pesaro, Helsinki, La Rochelle, Nantes, Munich, and New York. All of Adoor's films draw on the history and culture of his native Kerala. Kerala's transition from feudalism to modernity serves as a backdrop to his complex meditations on the psychology of power, the nature of oppression, the corruption of patriarchy, and the coexistence of the modern and the feudal in post-Independence democratic India. Elippathayam, his masterpiece, vividly captures the descent into paranoia of a man trapped within his feudal universe. In Mukhamukham, a study in failed idealism, a Communist leader gives up on revolution and decides to go to sleep instead. Vidheyan, a parable-like story, deals with the abuse of power, the plight of the outsider, and the nature of a master-servant relationship. The more recent films--especially Anantaram, Mathilukal and Kathapurushan--display a new concern with interiority and reflexivity, foregrounding time, memory, consciousness, and the nature of storytelling itself. Adoor's genius lies in his ability to create visually complex films that operate on multiple levels, that are culture-specific and yet universal in significance.

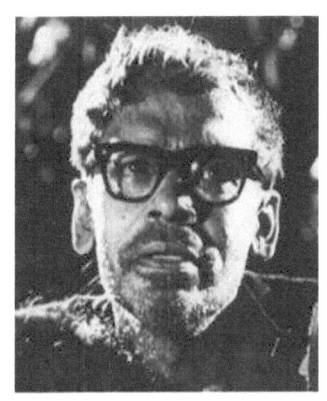

8.   **Ritwik Ghatak**

Ritwik Ghatak was a<u>Bengali</u> <u>Indian</u> <u>filmmaker</u> and <u>script writer</u>. Along with prominent contemporary Bengali filmmakers <u>Satyajit Ray</u> and <u>Mrinal Sen</u>, his cinema is primarily remembered for its meticulous depiction of social reality. Although their roles were often adversarial, they were ardent admirers of each other's work and, in doing so, the three directors charted the independent trajectory of <u>parallel cinema</u>, as a counterpoint to the mainstream fare of Hindi cinema in India. Ghatak received many awards in his career, including <u>National Film Award's Rajat Kamal Award</u> for Best Story in 1974 for his *Jukti Takko Aar Gappo*[4] and Best Director's Award from Bangladesh Cine Journalist's Association for *Titash Ekti Nadir Naam*. The Government of India honoured him with the <u>Padma Shri</u> for Arts in 1970.

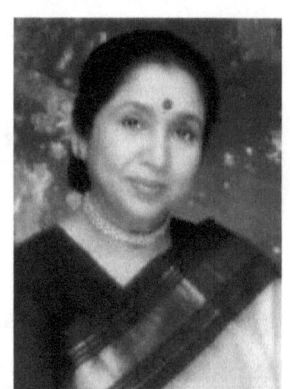

9.   **Asha Bhosle**

One of the greatest playback singers in Bollywood history, Asha Bhosle has recorded over 10,000 songs for over 800 movies. Although every class (ghazals, pop, etc) of song was within her vocal range, her specialty was in sensual songs or Western-styled songs--she had an uncanny knack for making every actress for whom she sung, fromZeenat Aman to Urmila Matondkar, smolder on screen as never before.

Born on 8 September 1932, Asha, like her sister, the legendary Lata Mangeshkar, was trained by her father, Dinanath Mangeshkar, in classical music, and it was only a matter of time before she too turned to playback singing. She made her debut with the film Chunaria (1948), but it took her a long time to make it to the top. Between 1948 and 1957, she sang more songs than any other playback singer, but the majority of these were in small, indistinct films--and whatever big film she got a chance to sing in, it was usually for the heroine's best friend or in a duet with bigger singers like Shamshad Begum, Geeta Dutt, or her own sister. And unfortunately having made an ill-advised marriage that alienated her from her family, she had no choice but to take up all available assignments to provide for her children.

However, in 1957, she got her big break with composer O.P. Nayyar in the films Tumsa Nahin Dekha (1957) and Naya Daur (1957). And 1958 saw the release of three of her films: Lajwanti (1958), Howrah Bridge (1958), and Chalti Ka Naam Gaadi (1958); their hit songs took Asha right up to the top. Thereafter, she became Nayyar's premier singer until the early 1970s, and they created musical magic together, particularly in the films Phir Wohi Dil Laya Hoon (1963), Mere Sanam (1965), Humsaya (1968), andPran Jaye Par Vachan Na Jaye (1974).

Initially Asha's singing style was initially reminiscent of Dutt's, but she soon overcame that and evolved her own distinctive style. Her voice possessed a lilting, versatile quality that could capture any song at any form or scale. By the end of the 1960s, she was second only to her sister, and the two of them were the queens of Indian playback singing right through to the 1990s. However, in spite of her incredible vocal range, she was getting typecast in singing sensual songs.

The 1970s saw her start a new relationship (which eventually became her second marriage) with composer Rahul Dev Burman - and so saw the birth of a great combination. A master of 1970s pop and disco music, Burman gave Asha a hip and happening sound altogether, and the two of them made their greatest hits with Haré Raama Haré Krishna (1971), Jawani Diwani (1972), Yaadon Ki Baaraat (1973), and Hum Kisise Kum Naheen (1977). Unfortunately, she again got stereotyped, this time in singing mainly Western-styled songs.

However, in 1981, the composer Khayyam revealed another, more lyrical quality to Asha's voice. Their collaboration in the Urdu film <u>Umrao Jaan</u> (1981), where the songs were mostly poetry, reveal some of her finest songs. And <u>Ijaazat</u> (1987), another such film, got her the National Award. Today, unlike her sister, she has remained active in playback singing--she still makes actresses sizzle in songs, most notably in the films<u>Rangeela</u> (1995), <u>Dil To Pagal Hai</u> (1997), and <u>Taal</u> (1999). She has also released several Indipop (Indian pop) music albums, and their success has reaffirmed Asha's.

Recently, she was nominated for the prestigious Grammy Award for Best Contemporary World-Music Album. Even at 70, there is no stopping Asha Bhosle....

10. **<u>Mrinal Sen</u>**

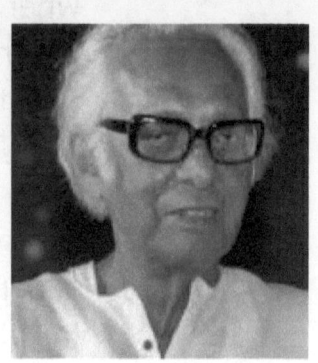

Sen is one of his nation's most politically active filmakers. After having studied physics at university in Calcutta, Sen worked as a freelance journalist, a salesman of patent medicines and a sound technician in a film studio. In the mid-1940s he joined the Indian People's Theatre Association and at that time began to read about and study film. The association had links to the Communist Party of India and this heralded the beginning of Sen's involvement with Marxist politics. In 1956 Sen made his debut with Raat Bhore(1956), the first of his 30 (as of 2002) films. Although his first film was openly political, he achieved national status as the director of a comedy, Bhuvan Shome (1969). Influenced by Italian neorealism and the work of fellow countryman Satyajit Ray, Sen used location shooting and non-professional casts in his early films. By the 1970s he was making wider use of symbolism and allegory. Although he remains politically committed, Sen feels that the "difference between party Marxists and a private Marxist like me is that others think they pocketed truth, whereas I am always in search of truth... " Sen's films have won numerous international awards. <u>The Case Is Closed</u>(1982), a scathing look at the hypocritical reaction of a bourgeois Calcutta family to the death of a servant boy, took home the Jury Prize from the 1983 Cannes Film Festival.

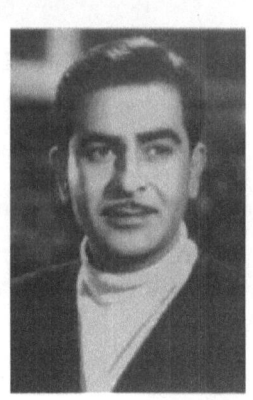

11.   <u>Raj Kapoor</u>

Raj Kapoor was the son of well-known Indian actor Prithviraj Kapoor, who acted both in film and on stage. After apprenticing in the Bollywood production studios of the 1940's, at 24 years of age Raj Kapoor produced, directed and acted in <u>Aag</u> (1948), with his new company, RK Films. His next production, <u>Barsaat</u> (1949), was a smash hit. In 1951, he also produced, directed and starred in <u>Awaara</u> (1951), which was another megahit, and costarred <u>Nargis</u>, who had appeared in Aag and Barsaat. Awaara also gained popular acclaim in Russia, where the movie and songs were dubbed into Russian. The theme song, Awaara Hoon, was popular in the East for many years. Kapoor has been dubbed "a great showman," and a filmmaker in the purest Romantic tradition, as he strove to entertain as well as address social themes close to his heart. Awaara dealt with the question of what forms an individual's moral grounding, ("nurture or nature") while incorporating comedy and stirring love scenes; in <u>Shree 420</u> (1955) he addressed issues of poverty, unemployment and national pride in the new Indian state at the same time maintaining the audience's interest in the romantic plot. While never revolutionary in tone, many of his films explore the ability of the individual to overcome economic and environmental injustice while maintaining his/her innocence and integrity. He is quoted as believing that the individual's struggles ultimately lead to the desire for love, to care and be cared for. This is consistent with his admiration of Charles Chaplin, and Kapoor's own "tramp" (Awaara, Shree 420, <u>Mera Naam Joker</u> (1970) is modeled somewhat on his mentor, though with a definite individual flair.

His films demonstrate an understanding of music and direction that continue to influence Bollywood filmmaking today. Also a musician, his understanding of the musical feel of his movies gives them a storytelling fluidity equal to that of the best American movie musicals. He surrounded himself with the foremost talents in filmmaking, acting, writing (Kwaja Ahmad Abbas'), music composition (<u>Jaikishan Dayabhai Panchal</u>, 'Shankarsinh Raguwanshi'), and playback singers, including <u>Mukesh</u>, 'Mohamed Rafi', and <u>Lata Mangeshkar</u>. Kapoor continued to make films of varying critical and popular success up until his death in 1988, and apparently considered Mera Naam Joker his personal favorite. He is still a well-known name not only in India, but in the Middle East, SE Asia, and Eastern Europe. His descendants have attempted to continue the RK Films banner.

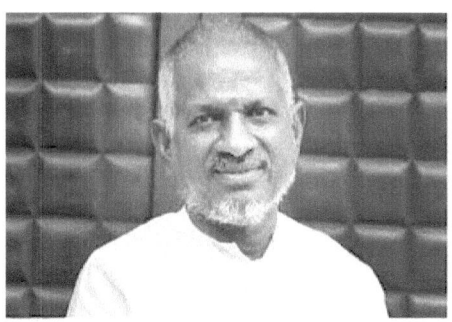

12.   **Ilayaraja**

Born and brought up in an obscure village near Kambam in Southern Tamil Nadu, Ilayaraja became the first Asian to score a symphony for the London Philharmonic Orchestra, besides scoring over 900 feature films in a period of 35 years. Raja, as he is popularly known and affectionately called, comes from a family of musicians. His mother, a huge repository of Tamil folk songs, seems to be a very strong influence in his music. He learned to play the harmonium, the typical musical instrument used in street performances. The team of the brothers, the eldest being Pavalar Varadharajan, a poet, worked as a group of musicians traveling across the state, accompanying theater artists. Raja picked up most of his acumen for audience tastes during this period.

In 1969, Raja migrated to the city of Madras, the Southern Movie capital, when he was 29 years old, looking for a break into music making for the public. He studied under Dhanraj Master, playing the guitar and piano in the Western style. He later earned a diploma in music from Trinity College in London. Ilayaraja's break into music for films came with <u>Annakili</u> (1976). The film dealt with a village story, to which Ilayaraja composed great melodies. The songs offered simplicity and musicality typical of Tamil folk in an authentic way, and they offered new sounds--rich orchestration typical of Western music. The songs became an instant hit, the most popular being "Machchana Partheengala" sung by a female voice, <u>S. Janaki</u>. This was followed by a series of films that portrayed contemporary Tamil villages in an authentic way, against stylistic shallow portrayals before. For all of these films Raja created memorable songs. Most popular were the songs "Senthoorappove" and "Aatukkutti Mutaiyittu" from <u>Pathinaru Vayathinile</u> (1977), and "Samakkozhi" and "Oram Po" from <u>Ponnu Oorukku Pudhusu</u>(1979).

Raja soon proved his abilities in other styles as well. classical Karnatic melodies were used in <u>Kannan Oru Kai Kuzhandhai</u> (1978) (Rag Mohanam), Mayile Mayile (Ragam Hamsadhwani), and Chinna Kannan Azhaikiran (Reethi Gowlai). Raja's grasp of Western classical structure became evident with his masterful use of the piano, guitar, and string ensembles. Some of the numbers that show his orchestral genius are "Pon malai Pozhudu" and "Poongadhave" from <u>Nizhalgal</u> (1980), Kanmaniye Kadhal from<u>Aarilirindhu Aruvathu Varai</u> (1979), "Ramanin Mohanam" from <u>Netri Kann</u> (1981), "En Iniya Pon nilave from <u>Moodupani</u> (1980), "Paruvame Pudhiya" from <u>Nenjathai Killathe</u>(1981), and "Edho Moham" from <u>Kozhi Koovuthu</u> (1982). These songs could literally be heard coming from every doorstep in Tamil Nadu state every day for at least a year after being released. Raja composed film music prolifically for the next fifteen years, at a rate of as many as three new songs a day. After a few years as a film composer, he could write all the parts to a score as they came to him, and his assistants would make fair copies, which would be recorded immediately.

Raja went for a trip abroad to Europe, partly to visit places where Wolfgang Amadeus Mozart, Johann Sebastian Bach, and Ludwig van Beethoven lived. They were his Manasika Gurus or non-physical teachers, he wrote once. He also met contemporary composers and arrangers including Paul Mauriat. His listeners were awestruck by the quality and quantity of his musical output. He also scored a few films abroad. Ilayaraja's image grew to be a unique one in the history of Tamil cinema: stories, themes, and castes would be changed to fit his music, which swept away the minds of millions of Indians in hundreds of films.

Ilayaraja also recorded non-film albums, such as "How to Name It" and "Nothing But Wind," which were well-received in India and abroad. In 1993, he wrote a symphony for the London Philharmonic Orchestra in an amazing one-month span. To many people who know him, Raja represents more than his music. He is a mark of great achievement that is possible by hard work, yet he is seen in most of his interviews as talking very philosophically. He is very much attracted by the philosophy of Ramana Maharishi of Thiruvanna Malai, who lived in the early 20th Century. Raja once referred to Ramana as "our Zen master."

13. Amitabh Bachchan

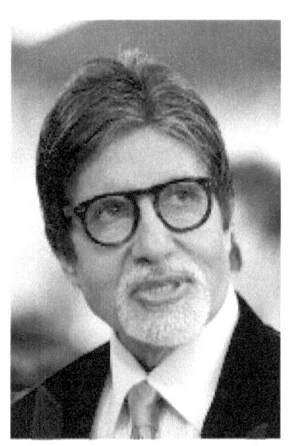

Amitabh Bachchan of well known poet <u>Harivansh Rai Bachchan</u> and Teji Bachchan. He has a brother named Ajitabh. He completed his education from Uttar Pradesh and moved to Bombay to find work as a film star, in vain though, as film-makers preferred someone with a fairer skin, and he was not quite fair enough. But they did use one of his other assets, his deep baritone voice, which was used for narration and background commentary. He was successful in being cast in Saat Hindustani. He got his break in Bollywood after a letter of introduction from the then Prime Minister Mrs. Indira Gandhi, as he was a friend of her son, Rajiv Gandhi. This is how Amitabh made an entry in Bollywood, starting with Zanjeer, co-starred with his future wife Jaya Bhaduri, and since then there has been no looking back.

He married Jaya Bhaduri, an accomplished actress in her own right, and they had two children, Shweta and Abhishek. Shweta is married, lives a non-filmy life and has two children.

Being friends with Rajiv Gandhi, got him to decide to run for seat in the Congress from his hometown but had to leave midterm because of controversies, particularly after Rajiv and he were implicated in the now infamous "Bofors" case along with the U.K. based Hinduja Brothers.

After a four year break, he was back in the unsuccessful Mrityudaata (1997), a comeback which the actor wanted to forget. Critics written him off but his career was saved with Bade Miyan Chote Miyan (1998). But four flops in 1999 and incurring debt of over 90 Crores rupees of his sinking company ABCL saw him at an all-time low. To make matters worse, after the defeat of the Congress party, Amitabh lost considerable political support, the opposition made him a target, and his credit rating deteriorated to such an extent that a leading nationalized bank, Canara Bank, sued him for outstanding loans. He did bounce back, presenting the Indian version of Who Wants To Be A Millionaire called Kaun Banega Crorepati? (2000). After a series of hits withMohabbatein (2000), Kabhi Khushi Kabhie Gham... (2001) and Baghban (2003) andKhakee (2004), this elderly Bachchan is showing no signs of slowing down and proving the critics wrong once again.

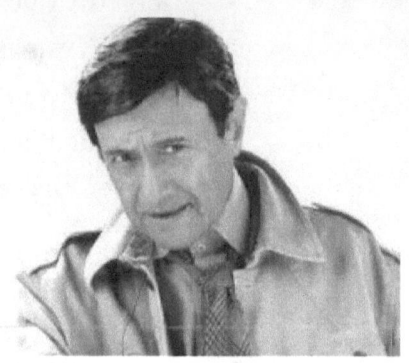

14.   Dev Anand:

After having played the Lead Actor for more than five decades in over 110 motion pictures, continues to bestride Indian Cinema today. He has given a new dimension to that magical state known as Stardom. And for his exemplary work he was awarded the Padma Bhushan in 2001 by the President of India. From the time he embarked on his career as a Film Actor in the mid-forties till now, his movies has been a journey filled with enriching experiences for the 'Evergreen Living Legend' of Indian Cinema. And he has always remained eternally youthful by his remarkable ability to live always in the present and the future; never in the past.

Also, as head of his film production company Navketan International Films, which was founded in 1949, Anand has introduced a multitude of talent to the Indian Film Industry by way of actors, directors, music composers and cinematographers. Today, he continues to introduce new talent to cinema and experiment with new ideas for movies. And today, he also heads one of the finest Film Sound Post-Production facilities in India - Anand Recording Studios - which has to its credit more than 3,000 Indian feature films that have been mixed/ surround mixed for worldwide release.

Anand has won two Filmfare Awards - India's equivalent of the Oscars - in 1958 for his performance in the film "Kala Paani" (Black Water) and in 1966 for his performance in Navketan International Films' "Guide". "Guide" went on to win Filmfare Awards in five other categories including 'Best Film' and 'Best Director' and was sent as India's entry for the Oscars in the foreign film category that year. He co-produced the English Version of "Guide" with the Nobel Laureate Pearl S. Buck ("The Good Earth"). Eventually, his creative sensibilities got the better of him and he started writing and directing his own movies.

In 1993, he received a Filmfare 'Lifetime Achievement Award' and in 1996 he received a Screen Videocon 'Lifetime Achievement Award'. Then in 1997 he was given the Mumbai Academy of Moving Images Award for his Outstanding Services to the Indian Film Industry. In 1998, he was given a 'Lifetime Achievement Award' by the Ujala Anandlok Film Awards Committee in Calcutta. In 1999, he received the Sansui 'Lifetime Achievement Award' for his 'Immense Contribution to Indian Cinema' in New Delhi. In the year 2000, he was awarded the Film Goers' 'Mega Movie Maestro of the Millenium' Award in Mumbai. And then in July 2000, in New York City, he was honored by an Award at the hands of the then First Lady of the United States of America - Mrs. Hillary Rodham Clinton - for his 'Outstanding Contribution to Indian Cinema'. And again Anand was awarded the Indo-American Association 'Star of the Millennium' Award in the Silicon Valley, California. The President of India honored Anand with the prestigious Padma Bhushan Award on India's Republic Day - August 15, 2001. And yet again, Donna Ferrar, Member New York State Assembly, honored him with a New York State Assembly Citation for his 'Outstanding Contribution to the Cinematic Arts Worthy of the Esteem and Gratitude of the Great State of New York' on May 1, 2001.

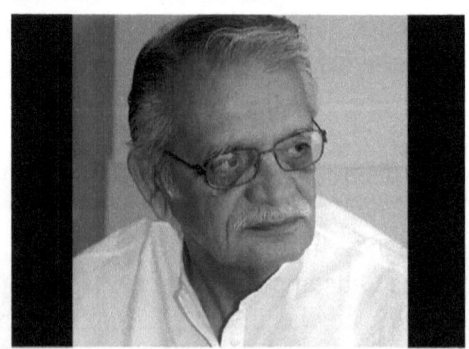

15. Gulzar

Gulzar is a writer, a lyricist, a director and, at heart, a poet. His films, sensitive, lyrical, and yet successful, were a welcome relief from the violent films that filled the 1970s and 1980s.

Born Sampooran Singh Kalra in Deena, in the Jhelum District in what is now Pakistan, he came to Delhi after the partition during independence as a poet. He joined Bimal RoyProductions in 1961 and got his first break as a lyricist writing for Bimal Roy's Bandini(1963). The success of this film made him Bimalda's full-time assistant and got him writing for films by acclaimed directors like Hrishikesh Mukherjee and Asit Sen. Some of the films he has written include Anand (1971), Guddi (1971), Bawarchi (1972), andNamak Haraam (1973) for Mukherjee; and Do Dooni Char (1968), Khamoshi (1970)

, and Safar (1970) for Sen.

Gulzar made his directorial debut with Mere Apne (1971). Based on Tapan Sinha's "Apanjan," the film looks at an old woman (played by Meena Kumari) caught between two street gangs of unemployed and frustrated youths. He then went on to makeParichay (1972) (loosely based on The Sound of Music (1965))
and Koshish (1972), which gave a superb look at the trials of a deaf and dumb couple (played by Jaya Bhaduri and Sanjeev Kumar). From this film came a mutually beneficial partnership with Kumar, which resulted in fine films like Mausam (1975), Angoor
(1982)Namkeen(1982), and the classic film Aandhi (1975),

which had been banned for a while. However, Gulzar didn't always depend on Sanjeev Kumar: the stars of the time, such asJeetendra, Vinod Khanna, and Hema Malini, worked with him in unglamorous roles and gave some of their best and introspective performances in films like Achanak (1973),Khushboo (1975), and Kinara (1977).

Musically, Gulzar was unbeatable. Being a lyricist and collaborating with film composers, he always had a high quality of music in his films, especially with Rahul Dev Burman. And while Burman became a pop icon with his tunes from Yaadon Ki Baaraat (1973) and Hum Kisise Kum Naheen (1977), he also gave Gulzar classic pieces with which to work in <u>Khushboo</u> (1975) and <u>Ijaazat</u> (1987).

Sadly, the 1980s and 1990s saw a decline in Gulzar the director, and although films such as <u>Lekin...</u> (1990) and <u>Maachis</u> (1996) had their moments, his last film to date, <u>Hu Tu Tu</u> (1999), was a misfire. However, he tried his hand at television with the much acclaimed television film <u>Mirza Ghalib</u> (1988). Made about the poet's life and starring<u>Naseeruddin Shah</u> in the title role, the serial was a landmark in Indian Television. Gulzar has also directed documentaries on <u>Amjad Khan</u> and Pandit <u>Bhimsen Joshi</u> as well as "Shaira," a film based on <u>Meena Kumari</u>. He has also turned his creativity into other channels--

he has written screenplays for films like <u>Masoom</u> (1983) and <u>Rudaali</u>(1993), and has written the lyrics for films like <u>Dil Se..</u> (1998) and <u>Saathiya</u> (2002).

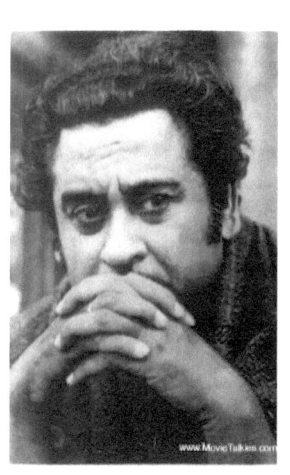

16. Kishore Kumar

Abhas Kumar Ganguly was born in Khandwa, now in Madhya Pradesh. His dad's name was Kunjilal, a lawyer by profession, and his mom's name was Gouri Devi, who came from a wealthy family.

Kishore was the youngest in the Ganguly family, preceded by Ashok Kumar, Sati, & Anoop Kumar (I). Sati was married to Sashadhar Mukherjee, who was the brother of film-maker Subodh Mukherji, and Bollywood actors Joy Mukherjee & Deb Mukherjee. Sati's son, Shomu Mukherjee, went on to marry Tanuja, and who subsequently gave birth to Kajol and Tanisha. Tanuja is the sister of Nutan, who, in turn, is the mother of actor Mohnish Bahl. Tanuja and Nutan are the daughters of the famed Shobhna Samarth. Sati was also aunt-by-marriage to Ram Mukherjee, who would subsequently marry and give birth to Raj Mukherjee and Bollywood actress, Rani Mukerji. Ashok's daughter is noted Bollywood actress, <u>Preeti Ganguli</u>, who is married to comedian and character actor, <u>Deven Verma</u>. Ashok's grand-daughter is actress, <u>Anuradha Patel</u>.

While Ashok went on to become a successful actor, Abhas, who was renamed Kishore, shunned acting, and preferred singing and mimicking <u>K.L. Saigal</u>. His brother, Anoop, while struggling to make a name himself, noticed this, and encouraged Kishore to sing in his own voice.

When <u>Sachin Dev Burman</u> happened to visit Ashok, he heard Kishore singing, and immediately signed him to sing for Bollywood movies. After Sachin's passing away, his son, <u>Rahul Dev Burman</u> took over and openly favored Kishore over other male singers.

He always wanted to be a singer, but acting was thrust upon him, and he did his best to live up to it. A Leo, Kishore was also known for his mad-cap comedy movies, and for his eccentricity as he used to 'talk' to his trees in his home, and had even put up a sign 'Mental Hospital' right outside his residence in Khandwa. He was also parsimonious, so much so that he was in arrears to the Indian Income Tax authorities, yet never missed a chance to make fun of them (Aur Peechey Pad Gaya Income Taxum, Jai Govindam Jai Gopalam).

When he refused to endorse

former Indian Prime Minister's 20 point Program during the 1975-1977 Emergency, he was banned from the Government-controlled media namely All India Radio and Vividh Bharati. Even duets with his voice were censored. He was not the only one in Bollywood, as others like <u>I.S. Johar</u>, <u>Dev Anand</u>, <u>Shatrughan Sinha</u>openly condemned Mrs. Gandhi's regime. After the emergency, her political party (Congress) was overwhelmingly ousted by the electorate in favor of the Janata Party.

Kishore made a record by being the only singer to have sung in more than 90 films for a single hero. Kishore sang in 91 films for <u>Rajesh Khanna</u>.His closest friends were Rajesh Khanna, R.D.Burman,

S.D.Burman, Mohammad Rafi.He refused to lend his voice to Amitabh Bachchan in period 1982-1987 many times, when the latter refused to do a guest appearance in a Kishore-produced film and this affected Bachchan's career as many of his films flopped post 1983.

His marriages to some of the most popular and attractive Bollywood actresses (Madhubala, Yogeeta Bali,Leena Chandavarkar) not only raised eyebrows, but added to his popularity.

He introduced his son, Amit Kumar, (sired from his first wife Ruma Ghosh aka Ruma Guha Thakurta) to sing, often along with him, and then amazed his fans by marrying widowed Leena Chandavarkar, who was just two years older than   Amit.

In the comedy, <u>Badhti Ka Naam Dadhi</u> (1974) a song 'Karne Chaley Thhey Shaadi Meri, Khud Ban Baithey Dulha', sung by Amit, hilariously chastised his dad for getting married, instead of searching for a bride for his son.

Through Leena he sired another son, <u>Sumeet Kumar</u>. Their marriage was intact until his unexpected passing on October 13, 1987, due to heart failure.

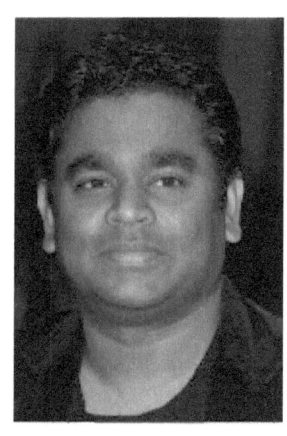

17.   A.R. Rahman

Allah Rakha Rahman was born A.S. Dileep Kumar on January 6, 1966, in Madras (now Chennai), India, to a musically affluent family. Dileep started learning the piano at the age of 4, and at the age of 9, his father passed away. Since the pressure of supporting his family fell on him, he joined Ilayaraja's troupe as a keyboard player at the age of 11. He dropped out of school as a result of this and traveled all around the world with various orchestras.

He accompanied the great tabla maestro Zakir Hussain on a few world tours and also won a scholarship at the Trinity College of Music at Oxford University, where he studied Western classical music and obtained a degree in music. Due to some personal crisis, Dileep Kumar embraced Islam and came to be known as A.R. Rahman. In 1987, he moved to advertising, where he composed more than 300 jingles over 5 years. In 1989, he started a small studio called Panchathan Record Inn, which later developed into one of the most well-equipped and advanced sound recording studios in India.

At an advertising awards function, Rahman met one of India's most famous directors,Mani Ratnam. Rahman played him a few of his music samples. Mani loved them so much that he asked Rahman to compose the music for his next film, Roja (1992). The rest, as they say, is history. He went on to compose several great hits for Tamil-language films before composing the score and songs for his first Hindi-language film,Rangeela (1995). The enormous success of his first Hindi venture was followed by the chart-topping soundtrack albums of films such as Bombay (1995) , Dil Se.. (1998), Taal(1999), Zubeidaa (2001), and Lagaan: Once Upon a Time in India (2001), which was nominated for best foreign-language film at the 2002 Academy Awards.

More recently, he worked with Sir Andrew Lloyd Webber and Shekhar Kapur (director ofElizabeth (1998)) on a musical called "Bombay Dreams." At 36 years old, A.R. Rahman has revolutionized Indian film music and one can only expect this musical genius to reach greater heights.

A two-time winner and five-times nominee of the Academy Award (Oscar), A. R. Rahman is popularly known as the man who has redefined contemporary Indian music. Rahman, according to a BBC estimate, has sold more than 150 million copies of his work comprising of music from more than 100 film soundtracks and albums across over half a dozen languages, including landmark scores such as 'Roja', 'Bombay', Dil Se', 'Taal', 'Lagaan', 'Vandemataram' and more recently, 'Jodhaa Akbar', 'Slumdog Millionaire', '127 Hours' and 'Rockstar'.

Rahman pursued music as a career at a very young age and after assisting leading musicians in India went on to compose jingles and scores for popular Indian television features. He also obtained a degree in western classical music from the Trinity College of Music, London and set up his own in-house studio called Panchathan Record-Inn at Chennai. In 1991, noted film maker Mani Ratnam offered Rahman a movie called 'Roja' which was a run-away success and brought nationwide fame and acclaim to the composer. The movie also won Rahman the Indian National Award for the best music composer, the first time ever by a debutant. Since then, Rahman has gone on to win the National Award 3 more times, the most ever by any music composer.

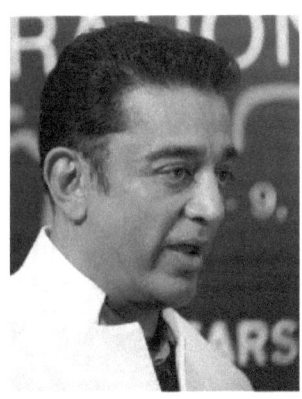

18. **Kamal Hassan**

Kamal Haasan was born November7, 1954 in Paramakudi, Tamil Nadu. He debuted as a child artiste in the film "Kalathoor Kannamma" (1960), which was released in the year 1960. Since then, he has starred in nearly 200 films in the major

Indian languages - Tamil, Telugu, Kannada, Malayalam and Hindi. He has been a part of the film industry for 52 years, as of 2012. His journey in cinema has seen him don various roles - from child artiste, to romantic lead to one of the most respected and revered heroes of the film industry today.

He has famously said that he is a reluctant actor. He has an avid interest in every aspect of filmmaking and is known for his work as a choreographer, director, and writer, as well.

He wrote his first script at age 18 for the film "Unarchigal" (1976), which was then followed by films that have gone on to become cult classics - Rajapaarvai (1981), Sathya (1988), Apoorva Sahotharargal (1989), Thevar Magan (1992), Mahanadi (1994), Kurudhippunal (1995), Avvai Shanmugi (1996), Hey Ram (2000), Pammal K Sambandam (2002),

Panchathanthiram (2002), Anbe Sivam (2003), are a few of the films etched in popular memory for having set the bar for craftsmanship in the fields of screenplay, script, and dialogue.

He is also a prolific writer of fiction and non-fiction in Tamil and his published work is testament to his constant exploration of structure and form.

Kamal Haasan's strong convictions in his art have led to some of Indian cinema's most path-breaking films like Pushpak / Pushpaka Vimaanam / Pesum Padam (1987). Kamal Haasan also worked as a choreographer while transitioning as a well-known child artiste to the lead actor in a feature length film. Some of his best-known work as a dancer can be seen in Saagara Sangamam (1983) and the popular hit Punnagai Mannan (1986).

Kamal Haasan is also a student of Carnatic music, studying under musical maestro Dr. Balamuralikrishna. One of his biggest hits as a playback singer was the song "Inji Iduppazhagi" for the film Thevar Magan.

His career as a director began with the film Chachi 420 (1997), the Hindi remake of Avvai Shanmugi. Since then he has called the shots for critically acclaimed films like "Hey Ram" and "Virumaandi".

He has never hesitated to state his opinions and encourage debate about topics that are socially relevant. He is a rationalist in thought and moderate in opinion and a humanist in philosophy. The need to be socially conscious is seen in the way his fan clubs have revamped themselves into entities that carry out charity and volunteer work.

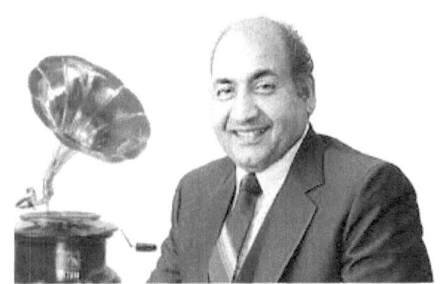

19.   Mohammed Rafi

Mohammed Rafi, whose voice
brought to life hundreds of
melodies, was born in a village
Kotla Sultan Singh near
Amritsar long before India
attained its independence. But
music training beckoned him
to Lahore where he cut his
musical teeth under the hawk-
like eye of Ustad Ghulam Ali
Khan. He made his singing
debut in the Punjabi film Gul
baloch by rendering a duet
with Zeenat Begum, 'Soniye Ni
Heeriye Ni' composed by
Shyamsunder.

Wadia Movietone was a

prominent film company and it was Homi Wadia who saw the talent in Mohammed Rafi and insisted that he sing for his forthcoming film Sharbati Ankhen under the Music directorship of Feroz Nizami. The voice of Mohammed Rafi encompassed a tremendous range, which is unparalleled. The peculiar trait that separates a playback singer from a classical vocalist is not the range or ability as a singer but the voice quality. With Mohammed Rafi it was the ultimate combination that helped him reign supreme in the field of playback singing. His voice quality combined with his unsurpassed range made him stand apart from his contemporaries.

His voice suited any genre of music be it a moving ghazal like Aap Ke Pehloo Main Aakar Ro Diye, a plaintive bhajan like O Duniya Ke Rakhawale, or a wild and whacky Shanker-Jaikishan composition like Chahe Koi Mujhe Jungle Kahe.

Mohammed Rafi added his delectable nuances to the melody and made it immortal. His voice had this unique feature of screen adaptability and when it merged with his intelligence as a singer it helped him to tailor his voice across an array of faces that remain entrenched in our memory books. Comedian Johnny Walker had a voice that was queerly rounded. Mohammed Rafi's take on him was phenomenal in songs like Sar Jo Tera Chakraye under S D Burman in Pyasa and Aye Dil Hai Mushkil Jeena Yaha from CID. Mohammed Rafi managed to sound exactly like Johnny Walker would if he sang the song himself. Rafi summoned Johnny Walker a day or two prior to the song picturization and then contributed his bit to add to the character Johnny Walker played on screen.

Honestly speaking it would not be in any way an overstatement to say that heroes like Biswajit (Pukarta chala hoon main), Bharat Bhushan (Zindagi Bhar Nahin Bhoolegi Woh Barsaat Ki Raat), Joy Mukherjee (Bade Miyan Deewane) are remembered more for the songs that were picturised on them with Rafi lending his golden voice to their average acting abilities.

Mohammed Rafi was known for his altruistic behavior, which was exhibited on several occasions. He has been known to charge just a token amount as his fees for singing songs of Music Directors who could not afford his regular charges. Many a times Mohammed Rafi has sung songs without charging a single penny to the Music Directors. A case in point is the film Aap ke Deewane with which actor Rakesh Roshan began his phase as a Producer-Director. Rafi sang the title song of the film but did not charge any money because he felt that he liked the song a lot and after all it was only a line, which he had to render. Very few singers were known to be so good at heart. This innate goodness in him came to the fore when he sang most of his songs.

In his glorious career Mohammed Rafi won the coveted Filmfare Award of best playback singer no less than six times. He was also decorated with the Padmashri by the Government of India. With the advent of Kishore Kumar as a major singing sensation Rafi sahab's career received a slight jolt in the late 60s and the early 70s but he bounced back with verve in films like Sargam, Karz, Hum Kisise Kam Nahin, Poonam and his last song under the baton of Laxmikant-Pyarelal for the film Aas Paas. He succumbed to the dreaded heart-attack on the 31st of July 1980 - ironically the man was a teetotaler and a non- smoker. He was in his mid fifties.

20.   Rajinikanth

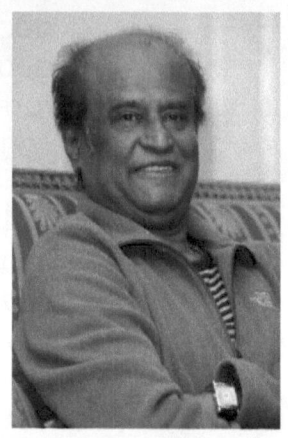

The Tamil mega star from 70s till present, he is one of the highest earning actors in Asia. He has also worked in Hindi, Telugu and Kannada and even an English film. Born in Bangalore (India) he was the son of a police constable. He was employed as a bus conductor before he joined the Madras Film Institute. He made his debut in <u>Katha Sangama</u> (1975) and became a star with <u>Apoorva Raagangal</u> (1975). His unique acting style is characterized by a trademark gesture: flipping a cigarette in the air and catching it in his mouth. His dark skin and heavy-lidded eyes have made him the hero of the lower classes. His fans conduct poojas on huge cutouts of Rajnikant just before the launching of his films to ensure his success.

His fans collect opening day ticket stubs of his movies and even buy them at exorbitant prices. Directors cannot 'kill off' his character in the movie for fear that the theatre will be burnt down to prevent future runnings of the movie by his 'crazed' fans who consider him almost a god. He is said to "explode like a tiger on screen".

Shivaji Rao Gaekwad (Rajnikanth) was born on December 12, 1949 in Karnataka. He was a bus conductor during which time he reportedly caught the fancy of the bus travelers with his mannerisms and style of issuing tickets and blowing the whistle and so on. Looking to become an actor, he moved to Chennai and joined the film institute. It was here that he caught the eye of K. Balachander, a director known for introducing talented, new faces into the tamil film industry.

Rajnikanth soon graduated to playing villains and his style, swagger and casually unique brand of villainy vowed the movie-going public. Be it the sadistic husband of Sujatha in Avargal or the wolf in sheep's clothing in Moondru Mudichu or the lust-filled village rowdy in Bharathiraja's 16 Vayadhinile, Rajnikanth was the villain the people loved to hate.

From here, it was a small step for Rajni, playing the anti-hero and finally, the hero in Bhairavi. Rajnikanth firmly captured the vacant, action-hero slot in tamil movies with a series of movies where he routinely bashed up the bad guys who had done him injustice in one way or the other. Once in a while he did movies like Aarulirundhu Arubadhu Varai or Johny which gave us glimpses of his acting potential. But action was what the fans expected from a Rajni movie and action was what he gave them. He has been superstar for the past 25 years.

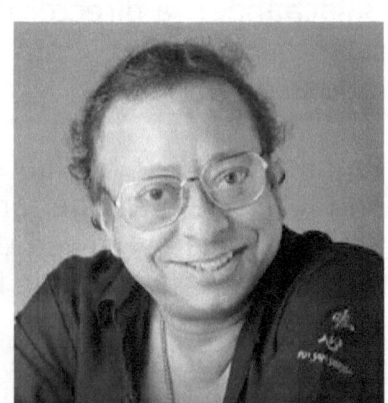

21.   **R.D.**

Burman

Rahul Dev Burman was an Indian film score composer, who is considered one of the seminal music directors of the Indian film industry.[Nicknamed **Pancham da**, he was the only son of the composer Sachin Dev Burman.

From the 1960s to the 1990s, RD Burman composed musical scores for 331 movies. He was mainly active in the Hindi film industry as a composer, and also provided vocals for a few of compositions.RD Burman did major work with Asha Bhosle (his wife) andKishore Kumar, and scored many of the songs that made these singers famous. In addition, he scored many timeless songs sung by Lata Mangeshkar. He served as an influence to the next generation of Indian music directors,and his songs continue to be popular in India even after his death.

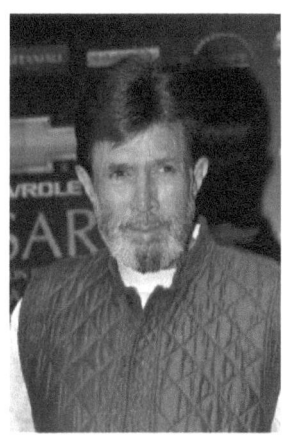

22. **Rajesh Khanna**

Rajesh Khanna, the first superstar of Indian and Hindi Cinema with 74 Golden Jubilee Hits - (which includes 48 Platinum Jubilee hits and 26 Golden Jubilee Hits) & in addition had 22 Silver Jubilee Hits and 9 average hits, was born on 29 December 1942 in Amritsar, Punjab, India.Rajesh entered Hindi films in the year 1965 when he began shooting for Raaz and did 180 films - 163 feature films and 17 short films. By 2011, he held record for maximum number of films as the solo lead hero and least number of multi star cast films in Hindi Cinema. Of the 163 films - 106 were solo hero films and 22 were multi star films and 29 films had him in special effective guest appearances(though only 97 solo and 20 two hero films only released and 11 unreleased from 1966 till 2013).He ranked first and won the United Producers All India Contest held in 1965 by beating 10000 candidates and the prize of it was acting in films Akhri Khat and Raaz. He first tasted success as an actor with 3 consecutive hit films like Aakhri Khat,Raaz and Aurat.His first brush with super-stardom was when outburst from his fans forced the director to change

the story of Baharaon Ke Sapne's ending
from a tragic one to a happy one after 1
week of its release. Though Baharaon Ke
Sapne was average in some centers it was
declared flop in most places. In 1969 Rajesh
Khanna achieved super-stardom with Shakti
Samantha's 'Aradhana" (1969).He became
the craze of the nation, and critics across
India started calling him the First Superstar
of both Indian Cinema (No. 1 Actor) and
Hindi Films and remained so alone as the
Superstar for 7 years (1969-1976) and had
to share the status with Amitabh from 1977-
1991 till he left films to join politics in
1991.He overtook his predecessors Dev-Dilip-
Raj, Shammi Kapoor,Rajendra Kumar in
terms of extreme popularity with audience
and critics, quality of performances, variety
of roles and films by doing quickly 47 films
from 1966-75 which included 36 Golden
Jubilee Hits(21 of the 36 were platinum) and
4 silver silver jubilee hits and only 7 flops in 9
years. He also made the world record of
having 17 successive super-hits in 3 years
from 1969-71 which included 15 consecutive
solo super-hit films and 2 two hero films
namely Andaz and Maryada. The main

difference between him and his predecessors,successors, contemporaries was that Khanna's films ran successfully in whole of India and not just Hindi speaking areas and he did films of every genre simultaneously and has more critically acclaimed films to his credit than all other Hindi Actors of every generation. He stands out even by selection of his films as he regularly did both offbeat alternate cinema along with commercial potboiler films and had success in both.He introduced intelligent cinema to the masses with ease. Those 15 consecutive hit solo lead hero films from 1969-71 were Aradhana, Doli, Bandhan, Ittefaq, Do Raaste, Khamoshi, Safar, The Train, Kati Patang, Sachaa Jhutha, Aan Milo Sajna, Mehboob Ki Mehendi, Dushmun, Anand and Haathi Mere Saathi. His next release Maalik flopped ending thereby the record.

Anju Mahendru was his girl friend in 1968-1972, the then aspiring actress but they had breakup in 1972 when Anju was not ready for marriage while Khanan wanted to marry her, and Khanna married his fan Dimple Kapadia in March 1973, 8 months before Dimple's debut film Bobby released in theaters.

Khanna's pairing with Mumtaz always produced much success as they had all of their 8 films together as major platinum jubilee hits.His films with Sharmila Tagore, Asha Parekh and Zeenat Aman was a favorite with audiences too in 70's.

From 1976 onwards till 1978, he had 5 box office hits as lead hero(2 silver jubilee hits, 2 platinum hits, 1 average hit), 3 hits in guest appearances, 1 flop in guest appearance and 8 films of him as the main lead flopped unexpectedly although his performances and the film's music were praised by critics and thereby 76-78 is considered his bad phase.

K.Balaji wanted to establish himself in Hindi film industry as a producer and thereby wanted to remake his Tamil film Sivaji Ganeshan starer Dheepam in Hindi. At a time when Khanna's films were not working at the box office, Khanna got this film out of the blue and went on to become a big hit. Khanna bounced back with twin success of

Amardeep and Prem Bandhan then again started giving many critically acclaimed and commercially successful films including 35 Golden Jubilee Hits(includes 25 platinum) and 14 SJH starting from 1979 till 1991 and had 9 average hits from 1976-1996. In the 80's his films opposite Tina Munim, Hema Malini, Reena Roy, Rekha, Shabana Azmi, Smita Patil and Poonam Dhillon were big hits.

He produced three films and co-produced 4 films. He had total 105 box office hits(91 as lead hero and 14 in guest appearance) from 1966-1991.He left film industry in 1991 and entered politics by joining the Congress Party in 1991 and became a member of parliament. Khanna was awarded Filmfare Special award in 1991 for having starred in 101 films as the solo lead hero(92 solo film released till 1992 and includes 7 unreleased solos and Anuraag) and having done just 21 two hero films(only 19 released till 1991) but having appeared in 153 films in short span of 25 years between 1966-1991. Has won most number of All India Critics Award for Best Actor for a record 7 times and was nominated for same 10 times.He holds record for being the actor to win maximum BJFA awards for Best Actor - 4 and was nominated the most for it - 25 times.He is still adored and fondly remembered by the masses. Songs from his films adorn the lips of youth and adolescents. He was the first mega-star and has left behind a storehouse of the finest moments in film history.

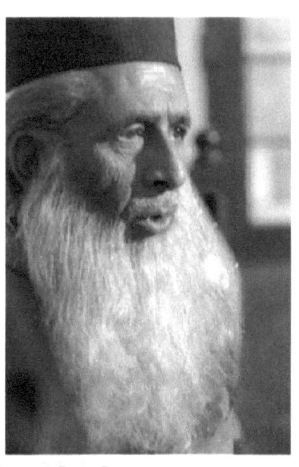

23.   **Naseeruddin Shah**

Naseeruddin Shah was born on July 20, 1950 in Barabanki, Uttar Pradesh, India. He is an actor, known for <u>The League of Extraordinary Gentlemen</u> (2003), <u>Monsoon</u>

Wedding(2001) and A Wednesday (2008). He has been married to Ratna Pathak since April 1, 1982. They have three children.

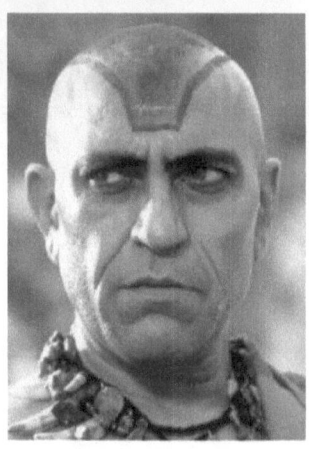

24.   Amrish Puri

Believe it or not, Amrish Puri wanted to become a Bollywood movie hero but failed a screen test in 1954. And what a failure it was! Mr. Puri went on to become one of the most renowned and credible villains in the history of Indian cinema. His most memorable and often quoted role is the character of 'Mogambo' (with the catchphrase "Mogambo Khush Hua"). It is still remembered fondly from <u>Mr India</u> (1987). <u>Shyam Benegal</u> cast him in movies such as <u>Night's End</u> (1975), <u>Bhumika: The Role</u> (1977), and<u>The Churning</u> (1976). <u>Yash Chopra</u> cast him in <u>Mashaal</u> (1984), the same year that<u>Steven Spielberg</u> cast him in his best-known role outside of India, as Mola Ram in<u>Indiana Jones and the Temple of Doom</u> (1984). His elder brother is none other than Bollywood actor <u>Madan Puri</u>. Amrish Puri died in Mumbai on January 12, 2005, due to a brain hemorrhage.

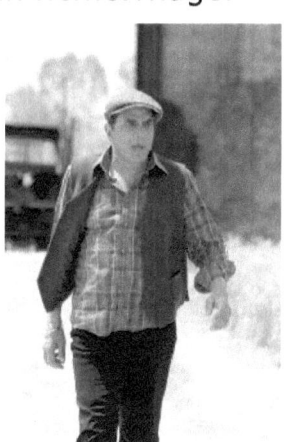

25. Dharmendra

He is one of the biggest stars of Indian cinema.

Dharmendra Deol played the romantic hero in woman centric films from 1960-1968 and became romantic hero from 1968-69 and played the role of action hero from 1975-1997 in A grade films. Dharmendra has appeared in almost 286 films. He is known as 'Garam' Dharam in Bollywood. He had the looks of a real gentleman, masculine body of a he-man and when it came to his films, he had a very humorous touch in his dialogue-delivery and the timing. Dharmendra's original name is Dharam Singh Deol. He was born in a Jat Sikh family in Phagwara in Kapurthala district in the Indian state of Punjab to Kewal Kishan Singh Deol and Satwant Kaur. He spent his early life in village Sahnewal and studied at Government Senior Secondary School at Lalton Kalan, Ludhiana. He did his intermediate from Ramgarhia College, Phagwara in 1952.

Dharmendra was fond of movies from a young age. He participated in the Filmfare new talent contest, which he won and came to Mumbai from Punjab looking for work. He made his debut with Arjun Hingorani's Dil Bhi Tera Hum Bhi Tere (1960). After which he got supporting roles in the film Boy Friend (1961) and was cast as the romantic interest in several woman oriented films from 1960-1967, where the story revolved around the heroine's character and, he was usually cast as a romantic hero opposite senior established leading actress of the time and later, from 1974 onwards, as an action hero. His major breakthrough was playing supporting role to hero Rajendra Kumar in Aaye Milan Ki Bela, where his character was negative and supporting role in patriotic film Haqeeqat (1964) and playing romantic interest in woman oriented films from 1960-1967 and playing supporting roles to Balraj Sahni,

Ashok Kumar, Biswajit in some films from 1960-67 like Soorat Aur Seerat, Bandini, Mamta, Ghar Ka Chirag.His sensitive side was explored by Hrishikesh Mukherjee in Anupama (1966) and Satyakam (1969), the latter is considered one of the best performances of his career. He got solo hero stardom with the blockbuster, Phool Aur Patthar (1966), which was his first action film but he became established action hero from 1971 film Mera Gaon Mera Desh. He cemented his image with successful films like Seeta Aur Geeta (1972), Raja Jani (1972), Jugnu (1973) and Yaadon Ki Baarat (1973). Dharmendra formed a popular onscreen pair with Hema Malini who later became his second wife. Hema Malini was the biggest female star of 1970s and the hit pairing with her was considered to be a booster for Dharmendra's career as they went on to star in hits such as Sharafat (1970), Seeta Aur Geeta (1972),

Raja Jani (1972), Jugnu (1973), Pratiggya (1975), Sholay (1975) among many others. Dharmendra proved his versatility and comic timing through Pratiggya, Chupke Chupke and Sholay. In Ramesh Sippy's Sholay (1975) he shared screen space with Amitabh Bachchan, Sanjeev Kumar and Amjad Khan and is still remembered for his inimitable portrayal of Veeru. His onscreen pairing with Amitabh Bachchan became extremely popular and they went on to star in more successful films such as Chupke Chupke (1975) and Ram Balram (1980). Their characters Jai and Veeru continue to remain the most popular "best friends jodi" onscreen. The song "Yeh dosti" picturised on both actors remains the most popular friendship song. Sholay became the biggest ever hit of Hindi cinema and created a record as longest running film in cinemas at that time when it ran for more than 5 years at Minerva cinema in

Mumbai. It became the first film to earn a Platinum Disc and is considered a classic (topping every must watch film list including Indiatimes 25 Must Watch Bollywood Movies). It was declared as Film of the Millennium by BBC and also awarded Best Film of Last 50 Years at 50th Annual Filmfare Awards in 2005. In mid- 70s, Dharmendra became the first Indian actor to be voted among the most handsome men in the world. Through the 70s and 80s, Dharmendra worked with some of the biggest names in B'town such as Bimal Roy, Yash Chopra, Raj Khosla, Ramesh Sippy, Rajkumar Santoshi, Hrishikesh Mukherjee and Basu Chatterji. In 1983, Dharmendra diversified into production and launched his elder son Sunny in 'Betaab', which was produced by his banner Vijayta Films and was a huge hit. in 1990, he produced Ghayal starring Sunny Deol in lead. The film was the second biggest hit of the year and won 7 Filmfare Awards including Best Film award and the coveted National Film Award for Best Popular Film Providing Wholesome Entertainment. He would later go on to launch the successful careers of his younger son Bobby in 'Barsaat'(1995) and nephew Abhay Deol in 'Socha Na Tha'(2005) under the banner. He has also periodically made films in his native tongue of Punjabi, starring in Kankan De Ole (Special Appearance) (1970), Do Sher (1974), Dukh Bhanjan Tera Naam (1974), Teri Meri Ik Jindri (1975), Putt Jattan De (1982) and Qurbani Jatt Di (1990). He continued to act in films through the 1980s and 1990s, though the films he did after late 80s were mostly in low brow action films directed by likes of Kanti Shah. Dharmendra was nominated 4 times for Best Actor Award at Filmfare Awards but never won. He was honoured with Lifetime Achievement Award by Filmfare in 1997. He made a comeback to A grade films with a role in Pyar Kiya Toh Darna Kya (1998). He joined politics and was elected as a Member of the Parliament in the 2004 general elections, from Bikaner in Rajasthan, on a Bharatiya Janata Party ticket.Dharmendra rarely attended Parliament when the house was in session. He returned to acting in 2007 with films Life in a... Metro and Apne were acclaimed and successful. In the latter, he appears with both his sons, Sunny and Bobby for the first time. His other release was Johnny Gaddaar, where he played a villainous role. In 2011, he starred alongside his sons again in Yamla Pagla Deewana released on 14 January 2011 and was a success. A sequel Yamla Pagla Deewana 2 was released in 2013. His also acted with his daughter Esha in his wife Hema Malini's directorial venture Tell Me O Khuda in 2011. In 2011, Dharmendra replaced Sajid Khan as the male judge of the third series of popular reality show India's Got

Talent. Dharmendra's first marriage was to Prakash Kaur at the age of 19 in 1954. From his first marriage, he has two sons, Sunny Deol and Bobby Deol both successful actors, and two daughters,Vijeeta Deol and Ajeeta Deol. He has 4 grand sons named Karan, Rajvir, Aryaman, and Dharam. Dharmendra fell in love with Hema Malini during the filming of Sholay. She eventually married him in 1980. As the Hindu Marriage Act forbade polygamy, he converted to Islam in 1979 to avoid protests and give legitimacy to his second marriage. The couple has two daughters, Esha Deol and Ahana Deol. Esha is an actress and Ahana is a dancer. Dharmendra has received several honours for his contribution to cinema and was awarded India's third highest civilian honour Padma Bhushan by the Government of India in 2012.

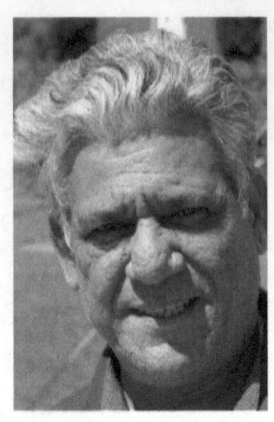

26.　Om Puri

Om Puri is an Indian actor who has
appeared in both mainstream Indian
films and art films. His credits also
include appearances in British and
American films. He has received an
honorary OBE.

Puri was born in Ambala, Haryana.
His father worked on the railways
and served in the Indian Army. Puri
graduated from the Film and
Television Institute of India. He is
also an alumnus of the 1973 class of
National School of Drama where
Naseeruddin Shah was a co-student.

Puri has worked in numerous Indian
films and in many films produced in

the United Kingdom and the United
States. He made his film debut in
the 1976 film Ghashiram Kotwal,
based on a Marathi play of the same
name. He has claimed that he was
paid "peanuts" for his best work. He
has collaborated with Amrish Puri as
well as Naseeruddin Shah, Shabana
Azmi and Smita Patil in art films
such as Bhavni Bhavai (1980),
Sadgati (1981), Ardh Satya (1982),
Mirch Masala (1986) and Dharavi
(1992). He has been active in
cinema. He was critically acclaimed
for his performances in many
unconventional roles such as a
victimized tribal in Aakrosh (1980)
(a film in which he spoke only during
flash-back sequences); Jimmy's
manager in Disco Dancer (1982); a
police inspector in Ardh Satya
(1982), where he revolts against
life-long social, cultural and political
persecution and for which he got the
National Film Award for Best Actor;
the leader of a cell of Sikh militants
in Maachis (1996); as a tough cop

again in the commercial film Gupt in 1997; and as the courageous father of a martyred soldier in Dhoop (2003). In 1999, Puri acted in a Kannada movie A.K. 47 as a strict police officer who tries to keep the city safe from the underworld - it became a huge commercial hit. Puri's acting in the movie is very memorable. He has rendered his own voice for the Kannada dialogues. In the same year, he starred in the successful British comedy film East is East, where he played a first-generation Pakistani immigrant in the north of England, struggling to come to terms with his far more westernised children. Om Puri had a cameo in the highly acclaimed film Gandhi (1982, directed by Richard Attenborough). In the mid-1990s, he diversified to play character roles in mainstream Hindi cinema, where his roles are more tuned to mass audiences than film critics. He became known internationally by starring in many

British films such as My Son the Fanatic (1997), East Is East (1999) and The Parole Officer (2001). He appeared in Hollywood films including City of Joy (1992), opposite Patrick Swayze; Wolf (1994) alongside Jack Nicholson; and The Ghost and the Darkness (1996) opposite Val Kilmer. In 2007, he appeared as General Zia-ul-Haq in Charlie Wilson's War, which stars Tom Hanks and Julia Roberts. He has worked in Hindi television serials like Kakkaji Kaheen (1988) (roughly meaning "Uncle says") as a paan-chewing 'Kakkaji', which was a parody on politicians, and Mr. Yogi (1989) as a suave 'Sutradhaar' who enjoys pulling the protagonist's leg. These two serials underlined Om Puri's versatility as a comedian. He received critical acclaim for him performance in Govind Nihalani's television film Tamas (1987) based on a Hindi novel of the same name. He essayed comic roles in Hindi films like Jaane Bhi Do Yaaro which reached a cult status, followed by Chachi 420 (1997), Hera Pheri (2000), Chor Machaye Shor (2002) and Malamaal Weekly (2006). His more recent Hindi film roles include Singh Is Kinng, Mere Baap Pehle Aap and Billu.

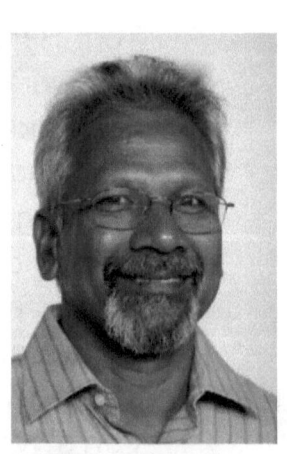

27.   **Mani Ratnam**

The man who revolutionized Tamil-language cinema, Mani Ratnam is the biggest director in south India and one of the most respected directors in all of India. Each of his films contain its own unique style, with beautifully photographed songs and unique backlighting. However, his films contain substance as well as style--Ratnam has dealt with a wide variety of topics, from the classic Indian love story to political thrillers.

He was born in Madras in 1956. Filmmaking was in his blood; he was the son of film producer 'Venus Gopalratnam' and his brother was G. Venkateswaran, a film distributor turned producer. Ironically, however, he studied at Madras University and received a management degree at the Jamnalal Bajaj Institute of Management Studies in Mumbai, and had initially started out as a management consultant. His first film, Pallavi Anu Pallavi (1983), starring Anil Kapoor, didn't make many waves, although it won the State Award from Karnataka that year, but even though he made two films in Tamil and one in Malayalam, nothing worked for him until he broke through with Mouna Ragam(1986). Starring Revathy, the film told the tale of a woman who, although forced into an arranged marriage, chooses to maintain a platonic relationship with her husband. The film was noted for its sophisticated approach and execution of an extremely sensitive topic.

His next film, Nayakan (1987), was also arguably his greatest. A take-off on Francis Ford Coppola' legendary The Godfather (1972), it established Ratnam as the leading director of Tamil-language Cinema and won its leading actor Kamal Hassan the National Award for Best Actor. The film draws on 30 years of Tamil Nadu's celebrity images and directly played to the anti-Hindi feelings of Tamil Nadu when the protagonist, beaten up, tells the Hindi policeman in Bombay, "If I ever hit you, you will die!"

Then came the best of his early work - Agni Natchathiram (1988), Gitanjali (1989), andAnjali (1990). The first was a tale of conflict between two step-brothers. Shot with glossy camera work, the film resembled a cross between an advertisement and a music video, and set a trend for a whole new visual style in Tamil-language Cinema. The next, <u>Gitanjali</u> (1989), shot in Ooty to create a soft and poetic mood, was a touching love story between two terminally ill people with less than six months left. The third,<u>Anjali</u> (1990), about a disabled child brought back to her family with two normal children had been chosen by India to be sent to the Oscars for Best Foreign-language Film, but it did not receive a nomination. The next year saw his first, and only collaboration so far, with the Tamil superstar Rajni Kant in the film <u>Thalapathi</u> (1991). It also starred Mamooty, along side a host of other actor. This star studded film was a gritty tale of an orphan who grows up to become a notorious gang member in Chennai. The story was inspired by the great epic of Mahabharata.

It was <u>Roja</u> (1992) that made Ratnam a household name all over India. A patriotic love story set against the backdrop of Kashmiri terrorism, the film was dubbed in Hindi and became a huge national success. It enforced Ratnam as a director of style and substance, as well as proving a highly auspicious debut for the now-acclaimed music director <u>A.R. Rahman</u>, whom Ratnam had discovered. It helped that India's at-the-time election commissioner T. N. Seshan took the rare step of officially endorsing the film.<u>Thiruda Thiruda</u> (1994), a remake of <u>Butch Cassidy and the Sundance Kid</u> (1969) was a misfire, but Ratnam bounced back with <u>Bombay</u> (1995), a politically charged romance between a Hindu man and a Muslim woman during the1993 riots in Mumbai. The film underwent some controversy due to its slightly anti-Muslim viewpoint, but it contributed widely to the success of the film.

Continuing his political obsession, Ratnam made <u>Iruvar</u> (1997), based on the MGR-Karunanidhi affair, and <u>Dil Se..</u> (1998), which starred superstars <u>Manisha Koirala</u> and <u>Shah Rukh Khan</u>. The latter was Ratnam's first Hindi-language film. Based on the northeast Indian problem, it told the story of a radio executive and a revolutionary. It had an excellent cast, beautifully crafted scenes, and most of all one of <u>A.R. Rahman</u>'s greatest tunes--but did not go down too well with the audience, who hailed it as a strange and confusing film that headed nowhere. However, today it is held as ahead of its time, being that it was shot pre-9/11, and is now hailed as a contemporary classic.

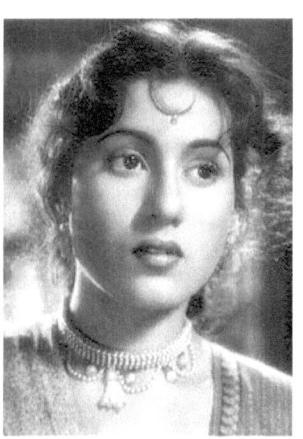

28.   **Madhubala**

Madhubala was an <u>Indian</u> <u>Bollywood</u> actress who appeared in classic films of <u>Hindi Cinema</u>.[2][3] She was active between 1942 and 1960. Along with her contemporaries <u>Nargis</u> and <u>Meena Kumari</u>, she is regarded as one of the most influential personalities of <u>Hindi</u> movies.[4] Madhubala has been called the <u>Marilyn Monroe</u> of India.[5][6][7][8]

Madhubala received wide recognition for her performances in films
like _Mahal_ (1949), _Amar_ (1954), _Mr. & Mrs. '55_ (1955), _Chalti Ka Naam Gaadi_ (1958), _Mughal-e-Azam_ (1960) and _Barsaat Ki Raat_ (1960). Madhubala's performance in _Mughal-e-Azam_ established her as an iconic actress of Hindi Cinema. Her last film, _Jwala_, although shot in the 1950s, was released in 1971. Madhubala died on 23 February 1969 after a prolonged illness.

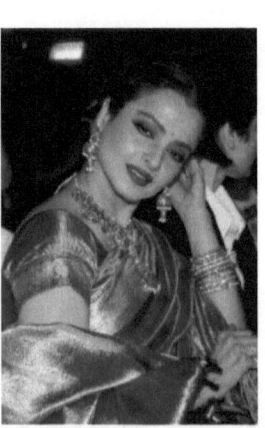

29.   Rekha

Bhanurekha was born in the Tamil-speaking Ganesan household on October 10, 1954. Her dad was the popular Tamil actor, Gemini, while her mom was a popular Telugu actress, Pushpavalli. She has seven sisters and one brother. One of her sisters is Dr. Kamala

Selvaraj, while another one, Radha, lives in San Francisco with a son named Naveed, who is being readied to act in Bollywood movies.

No stranger to the tinsel screen, Bhanurekha acted in a Telugu movie 'Rangula Ratnam' as Baby Bhanurekha along with her mom during 1966, which was subsequently re-made and released in Hindi during 1976 as Rangila Ratan (1976). She acted in one more Telugu as well as one Kannada movie (Amma Kosam and Goadalli CID 999 respectively) before re-locating to Bombay.

Due to her background, she ended up being very gloomy and pessimistic during her early years. She get a chance to debut in Bollywood movies during 1970 with Sawan Bhadon (1970) opposite Navin Nischol with a screen name of Rekha. Inability to speak Hindi, a dusky complexion as well as her weight did not exactly add to her assets in a predominantly fair-skinned, Hindi-speaking North-Indian film industry.

She decided to take matters seriously, took Yoga, shed those extra pounds, learned Hindi and dancing, and thus was born a new and much improved Rekha - who went on to deliver one box office hit after another for example <u>Nagin</u> (1976), <u>Muqaddar Ka Sikandar</u> (1978), <u>Mr. Natwarlal</u> (1979), <u>Khubsoorat</u> (1980), <u>Umrao Jaan</u> (1981), <u>Khoon Bhari Maang</u> (1988) amongst others. In her later years she has taken up character roles and appeared as a mother, even a grandmother in <u>Krrish</u> (2006) during 2006.

Her slim, slender looks got her many admirers, including well established Bollywood actors such as <u>Kiran Kumar</u>, <u>Jeetendra</u>, <u>Vinod Mehra</u>, and <u>Amitabh Bachchan</u>. Her marriage to Vinod ended in a divorce, and she ended up getting married to a businessman, Mukesh Aggarwal. This marriage also resulted in a divorce, with Mukesh killing himself shortly thereafter.

Must watch Bollywood Movies Before You Die

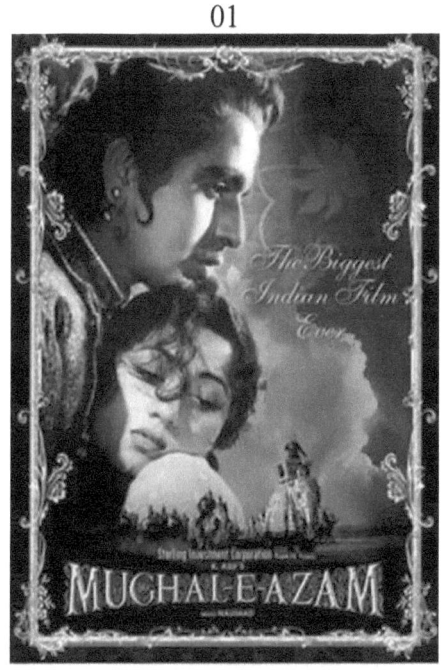

One of the most expensive films of Hindi cinema, 'Mughal-e-Azam' is considered as one of the milestone films in the history of Indian cinema. Directed by K Asif, the film casting Dilip Kumar, Prithvi Raj Kapoor and gorgeous Madhubala in the lead portrayed an eternal love of Mughal prince Salim and courtesan Anarkali.
Prithviraj Kapoor, who played the legendary role of King

Akbar, immortalised the character on celluloid. A poll conducted in 2013 by British Asian weekly newspaper rated it as the greatest Bollywood film of all time.

02

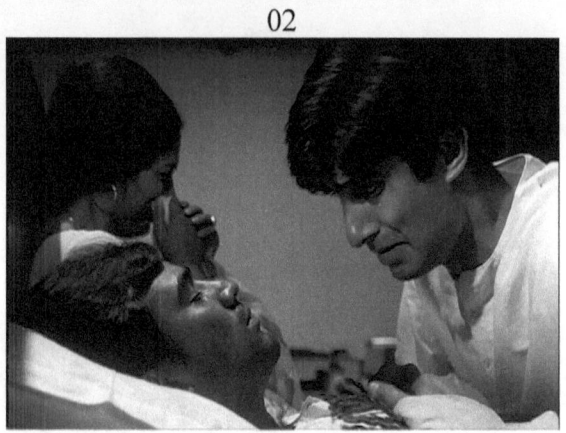

'Anand' was the cult movie of Indian cinema that proved Rajesh Khanna's -the first superstar of Bollywood- acting mettle. The film was story of a lively person suffering with a fatal disease passing every single moment cheerfully and bringing smile on every face. Rajesh Khanna and Amitabh Bachchan played their roles to perfection that brought tears on almost every eye when the movie ended.

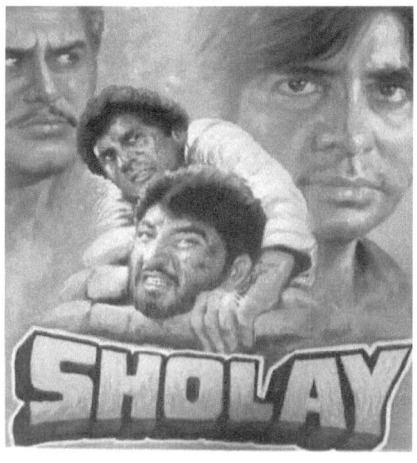

This is one of the most successful movies of the history of Indian cinema. With Dharmendra, Amitabh Bachchan, Sanjeev Kumar, Hema Malini, Jaya Bhaduri and Amjad Khan in the lead roles, 'Sholay' broke every box-office record and still as fresh and entertaining as its releasing time. The impact of the movie was such that every single character of the movie is remembered till date. And for the first time in the history of Indian cinema people loved the legendary villain 'Gabbar Singh' played by debutante Amjad Khan.

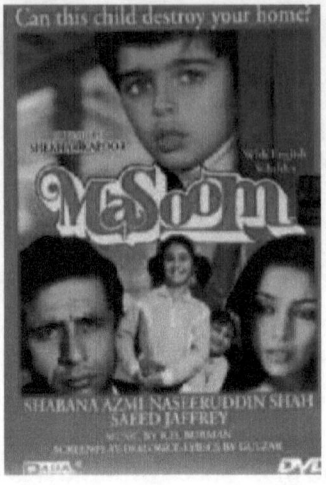

A cinematic gem from Shekhar Kapur, 'Masoom' touched every heart, kudos to Naseeruddin Shah, Shabana Azmi, and Jugal Hansraj (as a child artist) in principal roles. The film is one of the most acclaimed ones from that time and is the winner of many awards for its actors as well as for the people responsible for its timeless music- Gulzar (lyrics, screenplay, and dialogues), and R D Burman (music director). Shekhar Kapoor also won tremendous appreciation for his able handling of a sensitive subject in his debut directorial effort.

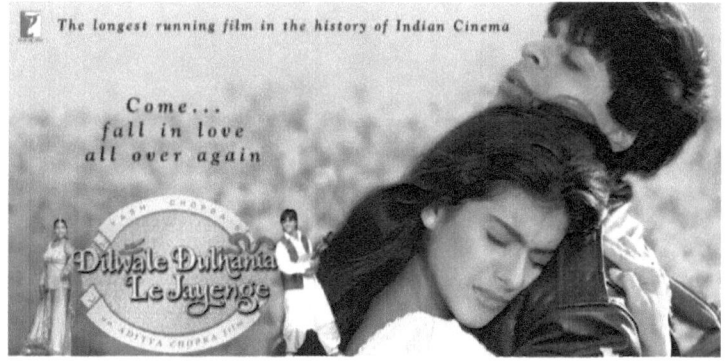

'Dilwale Dulhaniya Le Jayenge' gave another super star to the Indian cinema in the name of Shah Rukh Khan. The film once again brought back the era of love stories and introduced Indian audiences with the scenic beauty of Europe and desi land. After smashing many records at the box office, the film became the longest running film in Indian theaters after 'Sholay'.

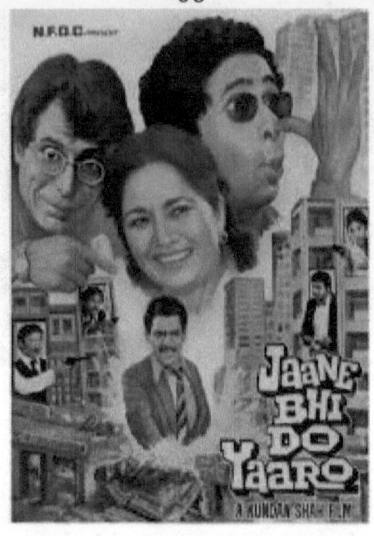

'Jaane Bhi Do Yaaro', with all its silliness, implausible plot and excessively theatrical acting, was an absurdist take on the builder-administrative mafia, which is still relevant now as then. Two bumbling jobless photographers are given an assignment by the hard-boiled editor of a newspaper whose sole goal is to catch the erring on the wrong foot. Like Sholay's dialogues, one has learnt JBDY's scenes and gags by heart - be it the cake scene ('thoda khao, thoda phenko'), the play on 'gutter', or the Mahabharat-Salim Anarkali stage mash up.

The hilarious jodi of Amol Palekar-Utpal Dutt and their rib tickling scenes together are still enough to make you laugh. It was also one of Hrishida's most famous and successful movies. Amol Palekar too earned a huge star status after its success. And of course, R. D. Burman also made his presence felt with the memorable song "Aane Wala Pal". In few words, 'Golmaal' is a brilliantly directed and intelligently edited masterpiece. Simply put, the movie is one of the key representatives of Indian comedies for rest of the world.

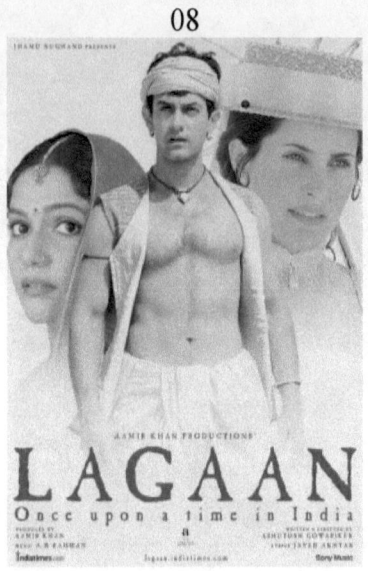

'Lagaan' was based on the story of a village that united against the British Raj to play cricket and achieve freedom from paying tax. One of the movies that re-introduced Indian cinema to the West, it was also voted in the top 5 films for the Oscars. However, the film failed to win the Oscars reason being its long duration but made a huge impact over the western audiences. 'Lagaan' also established Aamir Khan amongst the most versatile actors of Bollywood.

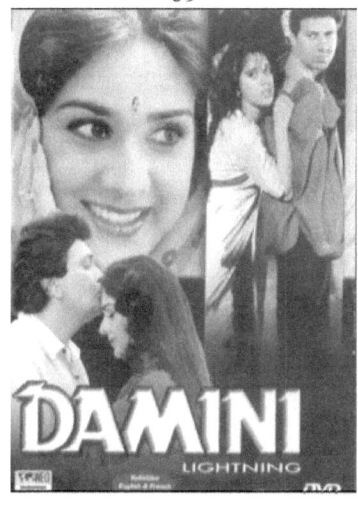

Raj Kumar Santoshi's 'Damini' was the tale of a small time stage dancer's struggle and fight for a poor rape victim. Powerhouse performances by Sunny Deol and Meenakshi Seshadri had earned them Filmfare. The conniving, evil scheming lawyer would be one of the best performances by late Amrish Puri. Santoshi's brilliant screenplay, his astute direction and punchy dialogues were the strong pillars of the film, which held it up high. The issues of domestic violence, raping a minor, judicial system all were very well reviewed and presented in the movie.

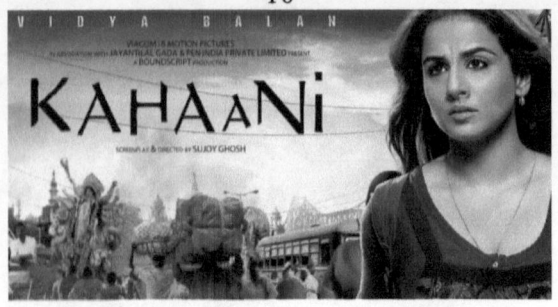

In 'Kahaani' Vidya Balan takes on her role with power
and pride. Living out of a suitcase, amongst strangers, she
takes on the soul of Kolkata. Her performance leaves you
in awe of an actress, who walks through her role as easily
as a stroll down Chowranghee Lane. And even that is
perfected as a pregnant waddle, add to it her disheveled
look and eyes dark with anguish. Sujoy Ghosh's script
and direction show no 'pregnant' pauses. It slams home a
shock value that a thriller rightly demands. The story
totally grips you and leaves you at a dramatic high.

Specially to Grateful to:

1. Vish Krishnan, History of indian Film and Music
2. Forbes India Magazine
3. Amitabha Bagchi, Role of Women in Indian Cinema
4. Amitabha Ray, Journey of women In Indian Cinema
5. Media India Group
6. CNN IBN'
7. Madhuja Mukherjee
8. Satyajit Ray, Our Films Their Films
9. Anupama Chopra